Introduction

Welcome to The Black Book of Instant Guitar Chords,
the ultimate chord reference book for rock, country, jazz and blues.

Inside you'll find all the chords you will ever need, described in
standard musical notation and as chord diagrams.
The chords are listed chromatically, so it's easy to
find the shape you need, and different voicings and
fingerings are given for every chord,
so that you can choose the shape that's best for you.

Chord families covered include:

- **Major**
- **Minor**
- **Diminished**
- **Augmented**
- **Add 9s**
- **Sus 4s and Sus 2s**
- **Sevenths**
- **Ninths**
- **Elevenths**
- **Extended jazz chords**

Plus special sections on:

Powerchords - all the essential powerchord shapes.
Slash Chords - useful chords with altered bass notes.
Transposing - how to move shapes around the fretboard.

This comprehensive collection is the perfect
reference source for the beginner or advanced guitarist,
and is designed to
be easy-to-carry and easy-to-use.

Instant Guitar Chords

Wise Publications
London/New York/Paris/Sydney/Copenhagen/Madrid

The
Black
Book

Exclusive Distributors:
Music Sales Limited
8-9 Frith Street,
London W1V 5TZ, England.
Music Sales Corporation
257 Park Avenue South,
New York, NY10010,
United States of America.
Music Sales Pty Limited
120 Rothschild Avenue,
Rosebery, NSW 2018,
Australia.

Order No. AM953414
ISBN 0-7119-7230-3
This book © Copyright 1998 by Wise Publications

Cover design by Pearce Marchbank, Studio Twenty
Printed in the United Kingdom

Your Guarantee of Quality

As publishers, we strive to produce every book to the
highest commercial standards.
Particular care has been given to specifying acid-free,
neutral-sized paper made from pulps which have not
been elemental chlorine bleached. This pulp is from
farmed sustainable forests and was produced with
special regard for the environment.
Throughout, the printing and binding have been
planned to ensure a sturdy, attractive publication
which should give years of enjoyment.
If your copy fails to meet our high standards,
please inform us and we will gladly replace it.

Music Sales' complete catalogue describes thousands
of titles and is available in full colour sections by
subject, direct from Music Sales Limited.
Please state your areas of interest and send a
cheque/postal order for £1.50 for postage to:
Music Sales Limited, Newmarket Road,
Bury St. Edmunds, Suffolk IP33 3YB.

How to use this book

The chord name is given at the top of each section, and the chord is then described in both traditional musical notation and as a chord diagram. Each chord has several possible voicings, which are shown from the lowest position on the fretboard to the highest.

The Chord Diagrams

The six horizontal lines in each chord box represent the six strings of the guitar:

The vertical lines represent the frets of the guitar. The thick vertical line is the nut at the bottom of the neck:

The circles on the fretboard show you where to put your fingers - a white circle indicates where the root note of the chord can be found:

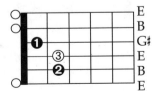

When shapes are played higher up the neck, the fret number of
the root note of the chord is given above the chord box.

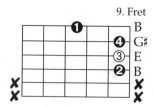

If a string is not played, an ✗ appears on the left-hand side of
the chord box; open (unfretted) strings are indicated by an O.
The sounding notes on each string are given on
the right-hand side of the chord box.

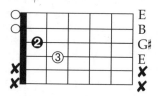

A bar is indicated by a shaded line crossing
the strings to be fretted.

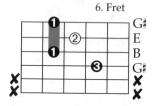

Example:

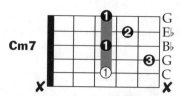

This chord box tells you to fret the top five strings
with your first finger at the third fret, placing your
second finger at the fourth fret on the second string, and
your third finger at the fifth fret on the fourth string.

The bottom string should not be played. It also tells you
that the sounding notes of the chord are C, G, B♭, E♭ and G, and
that the root of the chord is C, which can be found on
the fifth string at the third fret.

C MAJOR

C

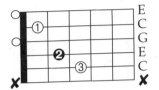
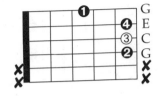
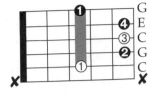

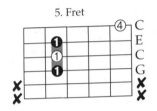
5. Fret

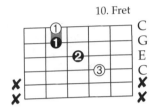
10. Fret

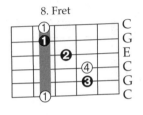
8. Fret

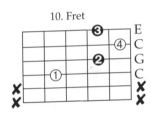
10. Fret

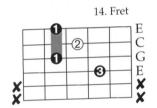
14. Fret

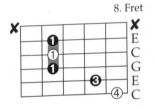
8. Fret

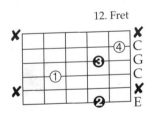
12. Fret

C
C#/Db
D
D#/Eb
E
F
F#/Gb
G
G#/Ab
A
A#/Bb
B
POWER CHORDS
SLASH CHORDS
TRANS-POSING

C

C♯/D♭

D

D♯/E♭

E

F

F♯/G♭

G

G♯/A♭

A

A♯/B♭

B

POWER
CHORDS

SLASH
CHORDS

TRANS-
POSING

C6

(no 5)

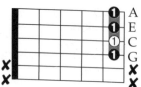

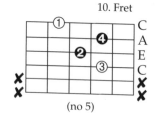

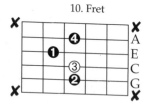

8. Fret

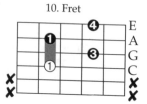

10. Fret

(no 5)

10. Fret

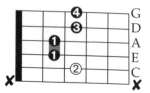

10. Fret

C⁶⁄₉

8. Fret

10. Fret

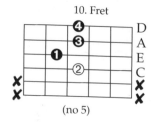
(no 5)

15. Fret

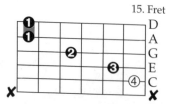

Cmaj7

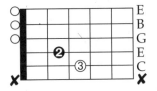

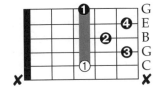

5. Fret

10. Fret

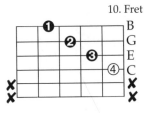

8. Fret

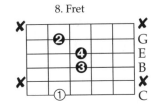

8. Fret

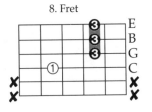

15. Fret

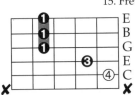

Cmaj13

8. Fret

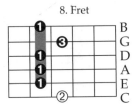

8. Fret

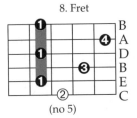

(no 5)

8. Fret

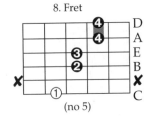

(no 5)

C

C#/Db

D

D#/Eb

E

F

F#/Gb

G

G#/Ab

A

A#/Bb

B

POWER
CHORDS

SLASH
CHORDS

TRANS-
POSING

Cmaj9

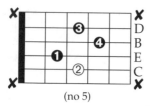

(no 5)

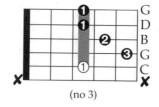

(no 3)

8. Fret

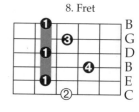

8. Fret

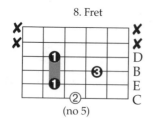

(no 5)

10. Fret

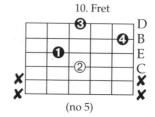

(no 5)

10. Fret

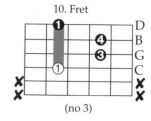

(no 3)

Cmaj9#11

(no 5)

3. Fret

(no 3)

8. Fret

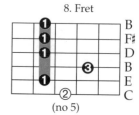

(no 5)

Cmaj7+

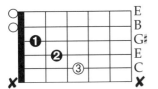

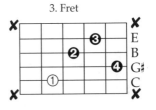

3. Fret

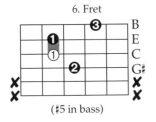

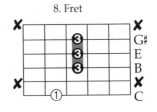

6. Fret

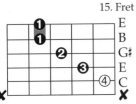

(♯5 in bass)

10. Fret

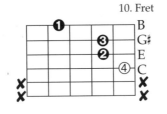

8. Fret

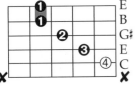

15. Fret

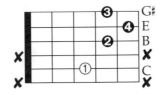

Cmaj7♭5

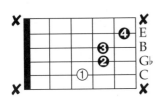

10. Fret

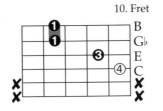

8. Fret

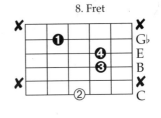

10. Fret

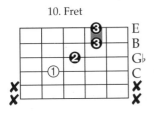

C
C♯/D♭
D
D♯/E♭
E
F
F♯/G♭
G
G♯/A♭
A
A♯/B♭
B
POWER CHORDS
SLASH CHORDS
TRANS-POSING

Cmaj13(no9)

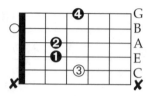

G
B
A
E
C

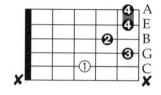

A
E
B
G
C

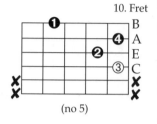

10. Fret

B
A
E
C

(no 5)

8. Fret

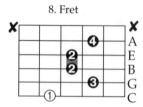

A
E
B
G
C

Cadd9

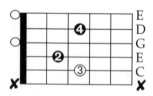

E
D
G
E
C

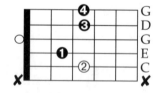

G
D
G
E
C

3. Fret

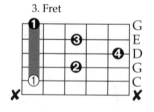

G
E
D
G
C

10. Fret

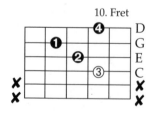

D
G
E
C

8. Fret

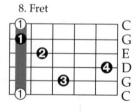

C
G
E
D
G
C

Navigation sidebar: C, C♯/D♭, D, D♯/E♭, E, F, F♯/G♭, G, G♯/A♭, A, A♯/B♭, B, POWER CHORDS, SLASH CHORDS, TRANS-POSING

Cm

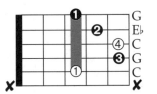

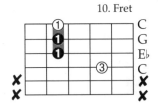

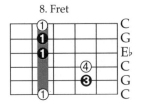

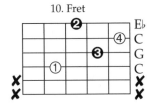

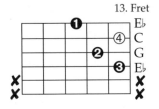

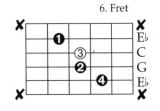

Cm7

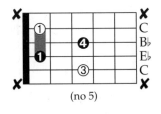

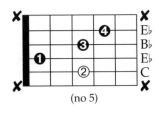

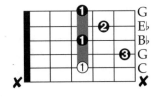

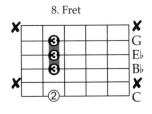

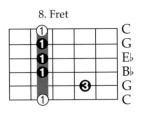

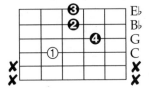

Cm6

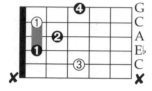
G
C
A
Eb
C

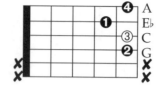
A
Eb
C
G

8. Fret

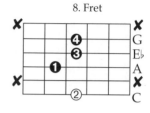
G
Eb
A
C

8. Fret

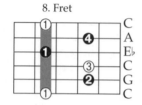
C
A
Eb
C
G
C

10. Fret

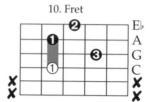
Eb
A
G
C

Cm(maj7)

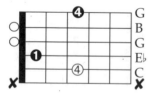
G
B
G
Eb
C

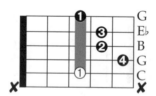
G
Eb
B
G
C

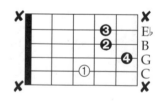
Eb
B
G
C

8. Fret

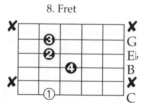
G
Eb
B
C

10. Fret

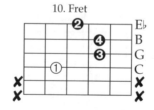
Eb
B
G
C

15. Fret

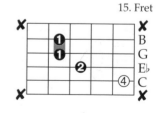
B
G
Eb
C

Cm add9

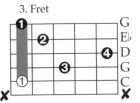

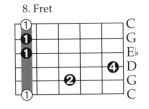

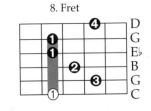

Cm9

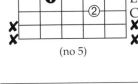

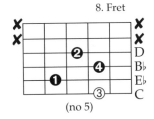

(no 5)

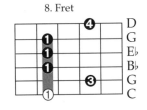

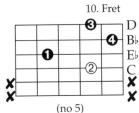

(no 5)

Cm(maj9)

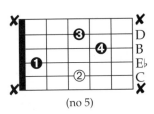

(no 5)

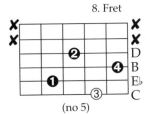

(no 5)

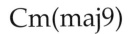

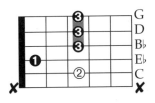

C
C#/Db
D
D#/Eb
E
F
F#/Gb
G
G#/Ab
A
A#/Bb
B
POWER CHORDS
SLASH CHORDS
TRANS- POSING

Cm $^6_9$

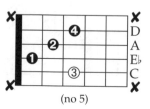

Cm11(no9)

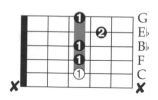

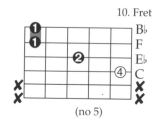

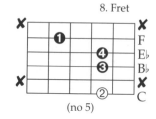

Cm11

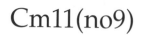

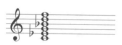

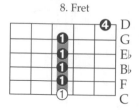

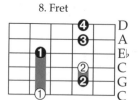

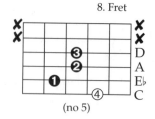

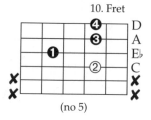

C7

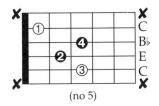

(no 5)

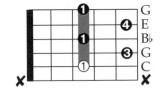

G
E
B♭
G
C

3. Fret

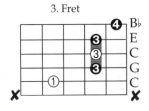

B♭
E
C
G
C

5. Fret

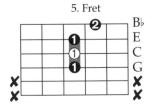

B♭
E
C
G

8. Fret

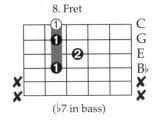

C
G
E
B♭

(♭7 in bass)

10. Fret

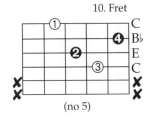

C
B♭
E
C

(no 5)

8. Fret

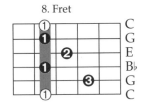

C
G
E
B♭
G
C

8. Fret

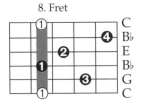

C
B♭
E
B♭
G
C

10. Fret

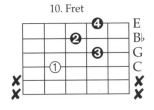

E
B♭
G
C

14. Fret

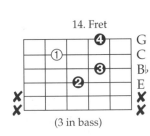

G
C
B♭
E

(3 in bass)

C

C♯/D♭

D

D♯/E♭

E

F

F♯/G♭

G

G♯/A♭

A

A♯/B♭

B

POWER CHORDS

SLASH CHORDS

TRANS- POSING

C9

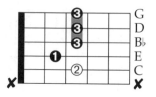

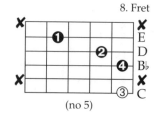
(no 5)

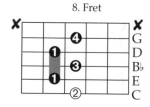

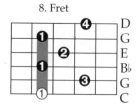

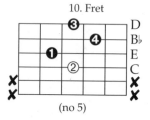
(no 5)

C13

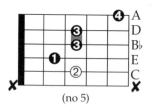
(no 5)

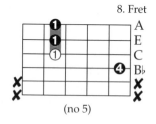
(no 5)

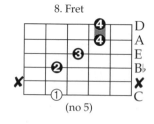
(no 5)

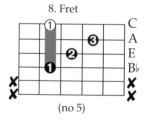
(no 5)

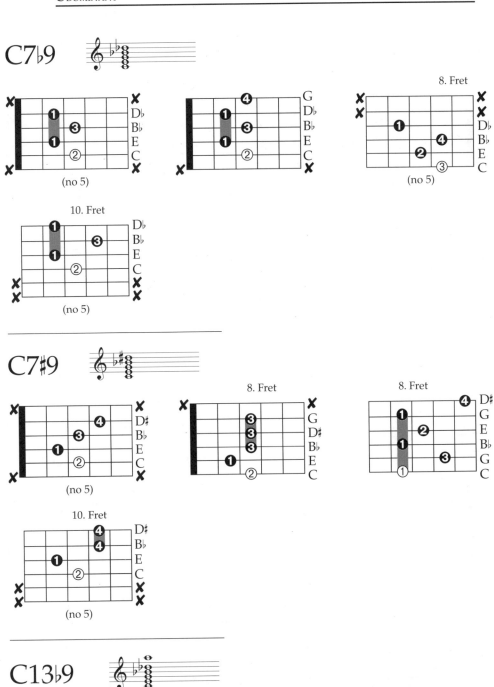

C7♭9

(no 5)

8. Fret

G
D♭
B♭
E
C

(no 5)

10. Fret

D♭
B♭
E
C

(no 5)

C7♯9

D♯
B♭
E
C

(no 5)

8. Fret

G
D♯
B♭
E
C

8. Fret

D♯
G
E
B♭
G
C

10. Fret

D♯
B♭
E
C

(no 5)

C13♭9

A
D♭
B♭
E
C

(no 5)

8. Fret

D♭
A
E
B♭
C

(no 5)

C

C♯/D♭

D

D♯/E♭

E

F

F♯/G♭

G

G♯/A♭

A

A♯/B♭

B

POWER CHORDS

SLASH CHORDS

TRANS-POSING

C7+

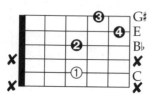

3. Fret

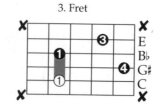

8. Fret

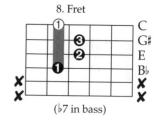

(♭7 in bass)

8. Fret

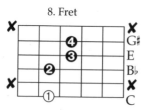

10. Fret

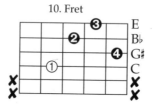

C7♭5

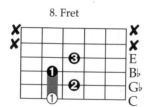

4. Fret

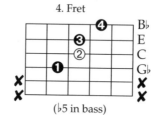

(♭5 in bass)

8. Fret

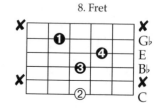

8. Fret

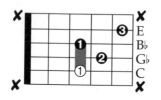

10. Fret

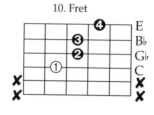

C7$\flat^9_{\sharp5}$

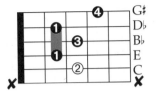

8. Fret

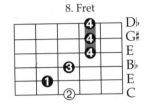

C7$\sharp^9_{\sharp5}$

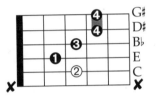

8. Fret

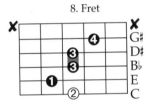

C9$\sharp$11

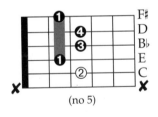

(no 5)

8. Fret

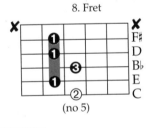

(no 5)

C9+

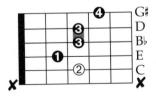

8. Fret

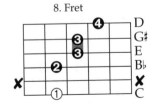

C
C♯/D♭
D
D♯/E♭
E
F
F♯/G♭
G
G♯/A♭
A
A♯/B♭
B
POWER CHORDS
SLASH CHORDS
TRANS-POSING

C
C♯/D♭
D
D♯/E♭
E
F
F♯/G♭
G
G♯/A♭
A
A♯/B♭
B
POWER CHORDS
SLASH CHORDS
TRANS- POSING

C7sus4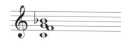

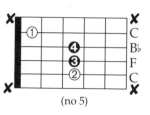

(no 5)

3. Fret

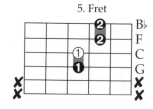

5. Fret

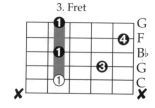

8. Fret

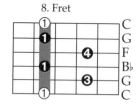

10. Fret

C9sus4

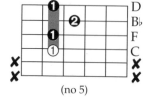

(no 5)

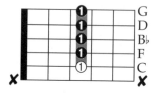

8. Fret

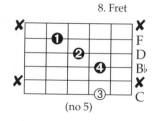

(no 5)

10. Fret

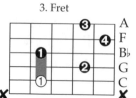

(no 5)

C13sus4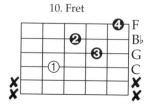

3. Fret

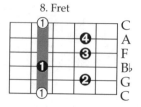

8. Fret

C°

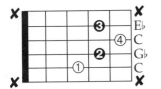

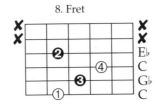

8. Fret

13. Fret

Cm7♭5

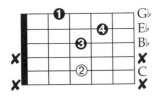

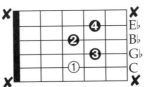

8. Fret

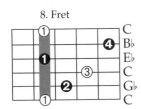

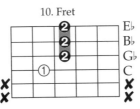

8. Fret

10. Fret

C°7

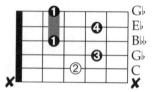
Gb
Eb
Bbb
Gb
C

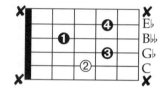
Eb
Bbb
Gb
C

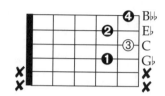
Bbb
Eb
C
Gb

7. Fret

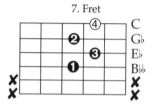
C
Gb
Eb
Bbb

8. Fret

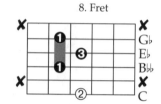
Gb
Eb
Bbb
C

8. Fret

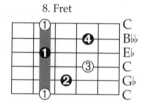
C
Bbb
Eb
C
Gb
C

10. Fret

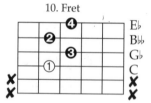
Eb
Bbb
Gb
C

C+

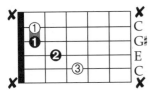

8. Fret

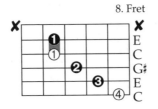

10. Fret

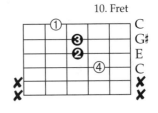

Csus4

3. Fret

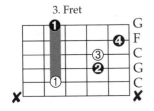

5. Fret

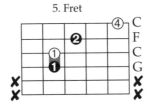

8. Fret

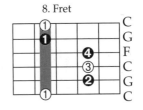

10. Fret

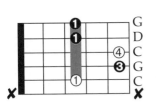

Csus2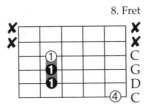

8. Fret

10. Fret

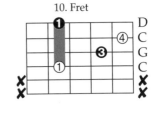

C

C#/Db

D

D#/Eb

E

F

F#/Gb

G

G#/Ab

A

A#/Bb

B

POWER CHORDS

SLASH CHORDS

TRANS-POSING

C#

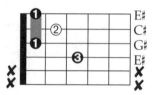
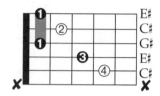
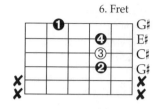

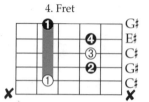
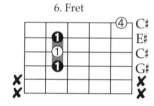
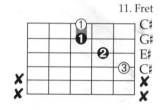

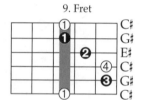
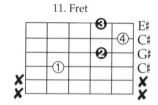
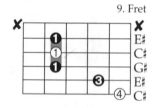

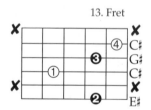

C♯6

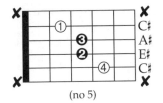

(no 5)

4. Fret

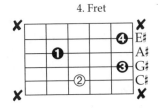

4. Fret

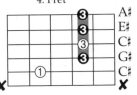

6. Fret

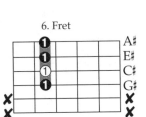

9. Fret

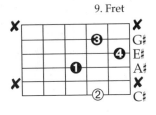

11. Fret

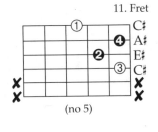

(no 5)

11. Fret

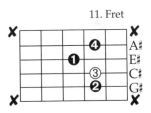

11. Fret

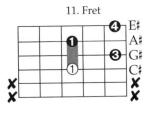

C♯ $^6_9$

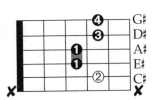

9. Fret

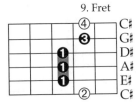

11. Fret

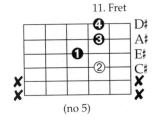

(no 5)

16. Fret

C♯/D♭

D

D♯/E♭

E

F

F♯/G♭

G

G♯/A♭

A

A♯/B♭

B

POWER CHORDS

SLASH CHORDS

TRANS-POSING

C♯maj7

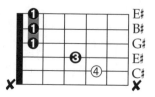

4. Fret

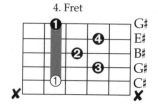

6. Fret

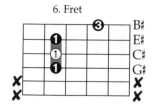

11. Fret

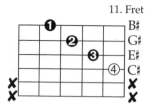

9. Fret

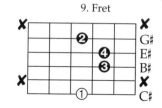

11. Fret

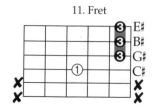

16. Fret

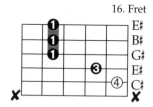

C♯maj13

9. Fret

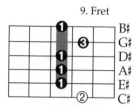

9. Fret

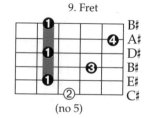

(no 5)

9. Fret

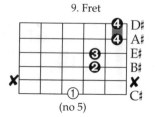

(no 5)

C♯maj9

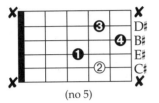

(no 5)

4. Fret

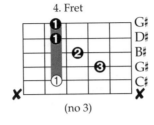

(no 3)

9. Fret

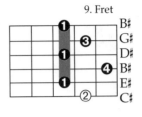

9. Fret

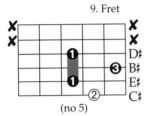

(no 5)

11. Fret

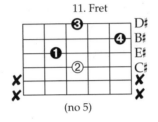

(no 5)

11. Fret

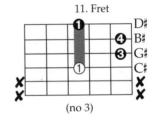

(no 3)

C♯maj9♯11

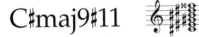

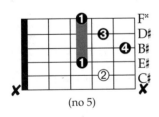

(no 5)

4. Fret

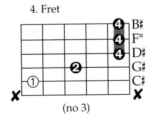

(no 3)

9. Fret

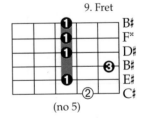

(no 5)

C

C♯/D♭

D

D♯/E♭

E

F

F♯/G♭

G

G♯/A♭

A

A♯/B♭

B

POWER CHORDS

SLASH CHORDS

TRANS-POSING

C♯maj7+

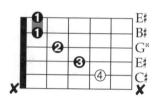

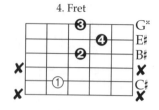
4. Fret

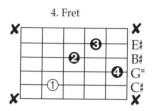
4. Fret

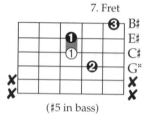
7. Fret

(♯5 in bass)

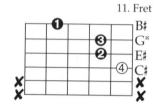
11. Fret

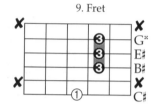
9. Fret

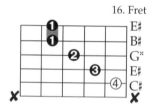
16. Fret

C♯maj7♭5

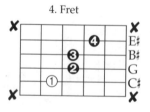
4. Fret

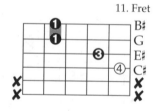
11. Fret

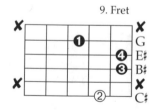
9. Fret

11. Fret

C♯maj13(no9)

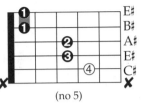

E♯
B♯
A♯
E♯
C♯

(no 5)

4. Fret

A♯
E♯
B♯
G♯
C♯

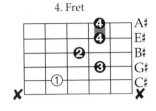

11. Fret

B♯
A♯
E♯
C♯

(no 5)

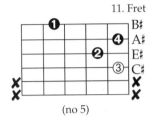

9. Fret

A♯
E♯
B♯
G♯
C♯

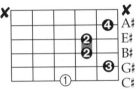

C♯add9

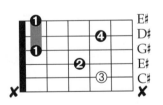

E♯
D♯
G♯
E♯
C♯

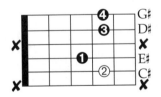

G♯
D♯

E♯
C♯

4. Fret

G♯
E♯
D♯
G♯
C♯

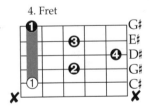

11. Fret

D♯
G♯
E♯
C♯

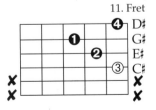

9. Fret

C♯
G♯
E♯
D♯
G♯
C♯

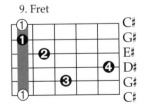

C
C♯/D♭
D
D♯/E♭
E
F
F♯/G♭
G
G♯/A♭
A
A♯/B♭
B
POWER CHORDS
SLASH CHORDS
TRANS-POSING

C♯m

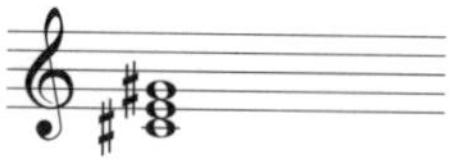

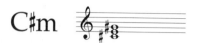

4. Fret

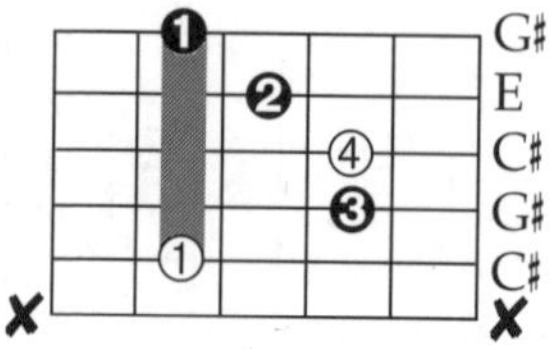
G♯
E
C♯
G♯
C♯

11. Fret

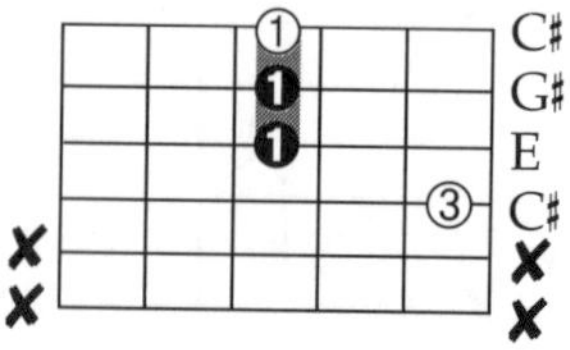
C♯
G♯
E
C♯

9. Fret

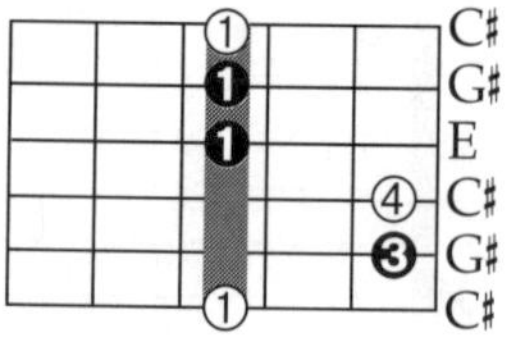
C♯
G♯
E
C♯
G♯
C♯

11. Fret

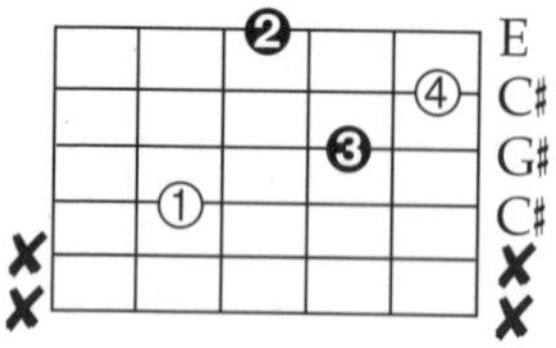
E
C♯
G♯
C♯

14. Fret

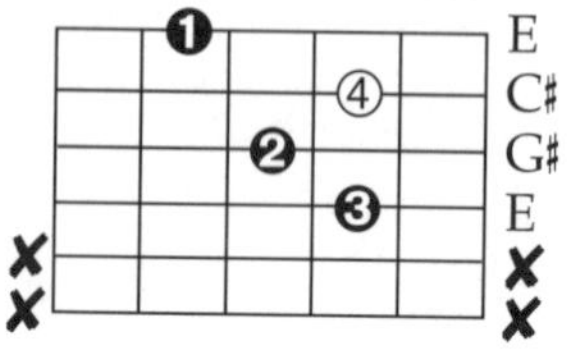
E
C♯
G♯
E

7. Fret

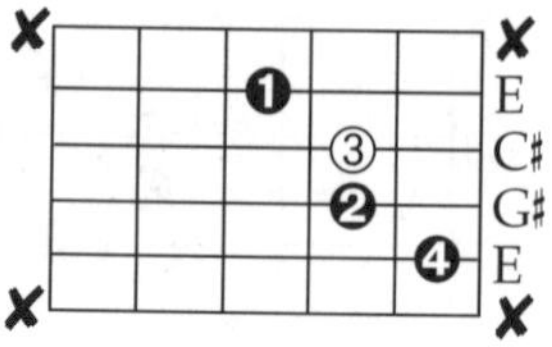
E
C♯
G♯
E

C♯m7

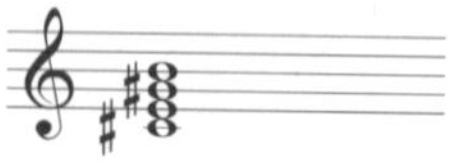

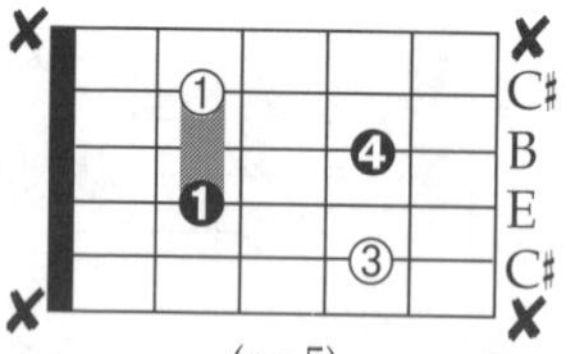
C♯
B
E
C♯

(no 5)

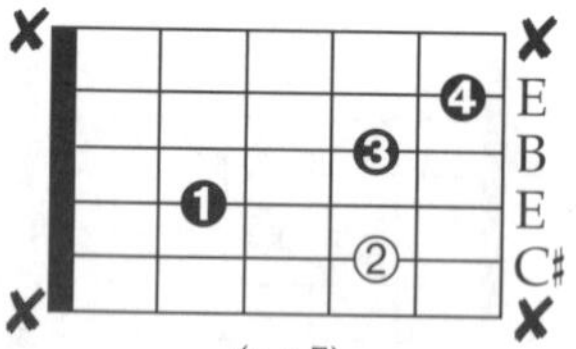
E
B
E
C♯

(no 5)

4. Fret

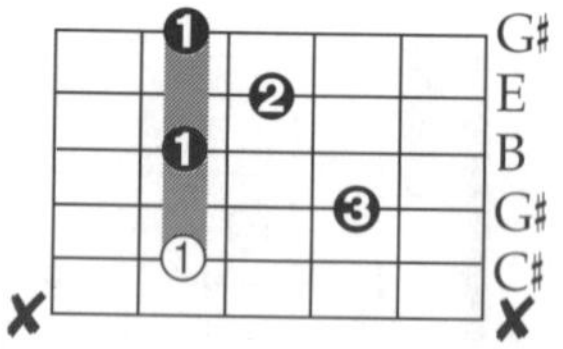
G♯
E
B
G♯
C♯

9. Fret

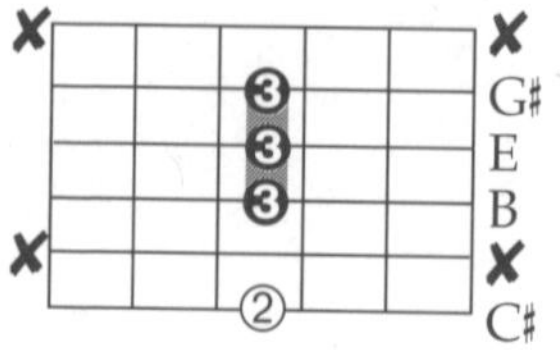
G♯
E
B
C♯

9. Fret

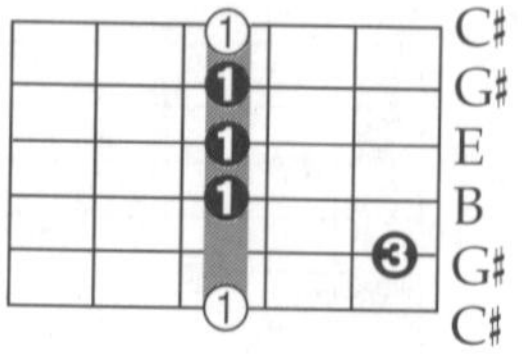
C♯
G♯
E
B
G♯
C♯

11. Fret

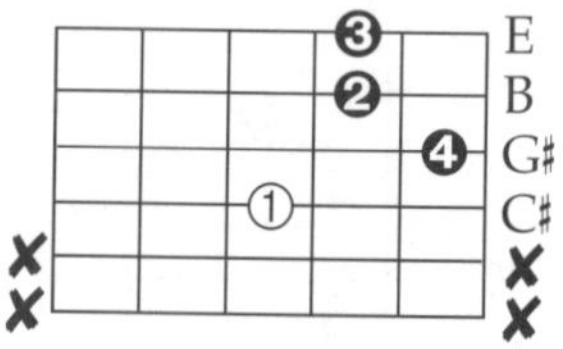
E
B
G♯
C♯

C♯m6

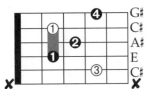

6. Fret

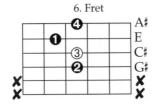

9. Fret

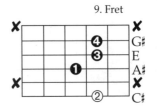

9. Fret

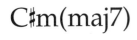

11. Fret

C♯m(maj7)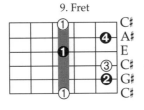

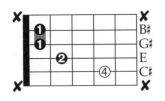

4. Fret

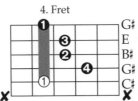

4. Fret

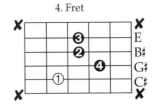

9. Fret

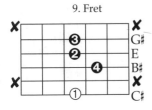

11. Fret

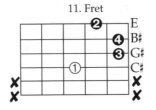

16. Fret

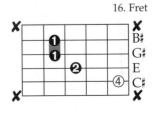

C

C♯/D♭

D

D♯/E♭

E

F

F♯/G♭

G

G♯/A♭

A

A♯/B♭

B

POWER
CHORDS

SLASH
CHORDS

TRANS-
POSING

C♯m add9

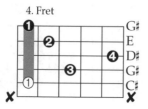
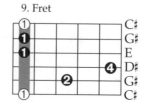
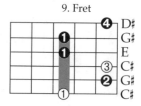

C♯m9

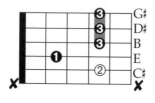
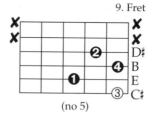
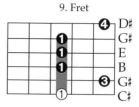

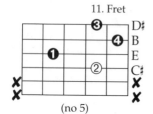

C♯m(maj9)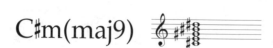

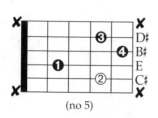
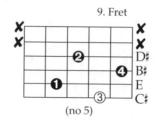
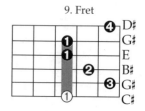

C♯m$^6_9$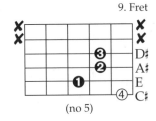

(no 5)

9. Fret

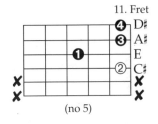

(no 5)

11. Fret

(no 5)

9. Fret

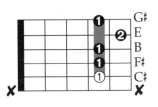

C♯m11(no9)

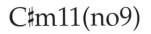

11. Fret

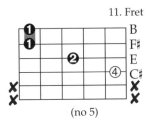

(no 5)

9. Fret

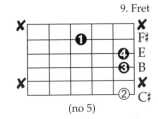

(no 5)

C♯m11

9. Fret

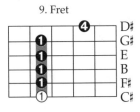

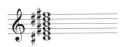

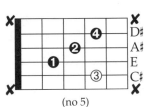

C♯7

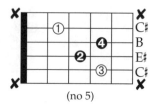
(no 5)

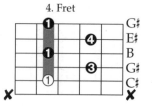
4. Fret

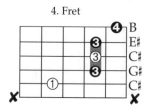
4. Fret

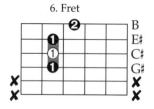

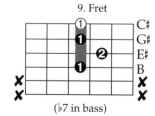
9. Fret
(♭7 in bass)

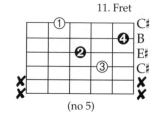

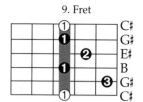

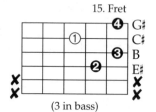
6. Fret

9. Fret

11. Fret
(no 5)

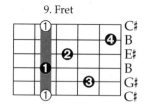

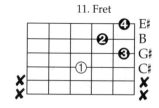

9. Fret

9. Fret

11. Fret

15. Fret
(3 in bass)

C♯9

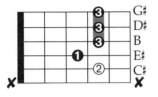

9. Fret
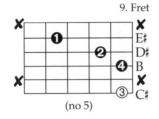
(no 5)

9. Fret
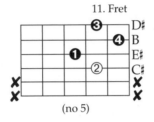

9. Fret
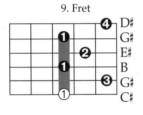

11. Fret
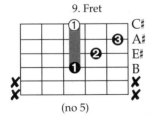
(no 5)

C♯13

4. Fret
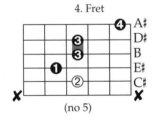
(no 5)

9. Fret
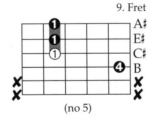
(no 5)

9. Fret
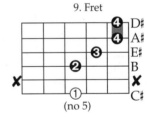
(no 5)

9. Fret

(no 5)

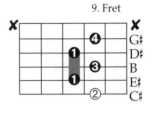

C♯7♭9

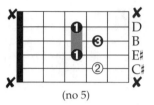

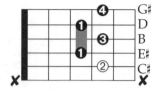

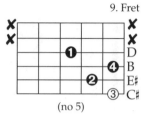

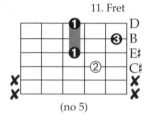

C♯7♯9

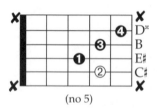

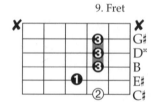

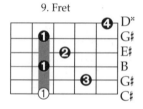

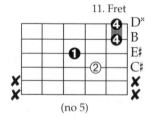

C♯13♭9

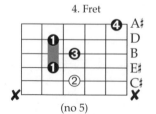

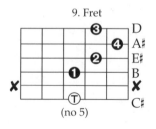

C♯7+

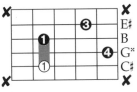

4. Fret
X X
E♯
B
G×
C♯
X

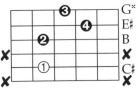

4. Fret
G×
E♯
B
X
C♯
X

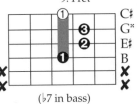

9. Fret
C♯
G×
E♯
B
X
X

(♭7 in bass)

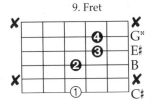

9. Fret
X X
G×
E♯
B
X
C♯

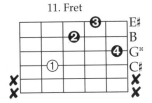

11. Fret
E♯
B
G×
C♯
X
X

C♯7♭5

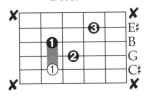

4. Fret
X X
E♯
B
G
C♯
X

5. Fret
B
E♯
C♯
G
X
X

(♭5 in bass)

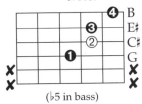

9. Fret
X X
G
E♯
B
X
C♯

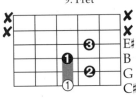

9. Fret
X X
X
E♯
B
G
C♯

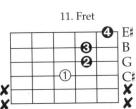

11. Fret
E♯
B
G
C♯
X
X

C

C♯/D♭

D

D♯/E♭

E

F

F♯/G♭

G

G♯/A♭

A

A♯/B♭

B

POWER CHORDS

SLASH CHORDS

TRANS- POSING

C C♯/D♭ D D♯/E♭ E F F♯/G♭ G G♯/A♭ A A♯/B♭ B POWER CHORDS SLASH CHORDS TRANS- POSING

C♯7 ♭9♯5

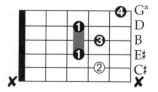

G×
D
B
E♯
C♯

9. Fret

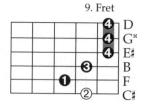

D
G×
E♯
B
F
C♯

C♯7 ♯9♯5

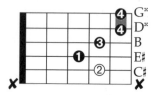

G×
D×
B
E♯
C♯

9. Fret

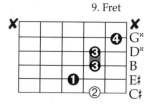

G×
D×
B
E♯
C♯

C♯9♯11

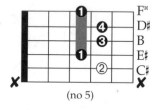

F×
D♯
B
E♯
C♯

(no 5)

9. Fret

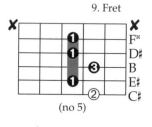

F×
D♯
B
E♯
C♯

(no 5)

C♯9+

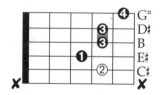

G×
D♯
B
E♯
C♯

9. Fret

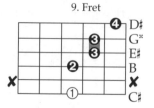

D♯
G×
E♯
B
C♯

C♯7sus4

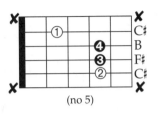

(no 5)

4. Fret

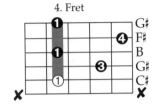

6. Fret

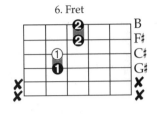

9. Fret

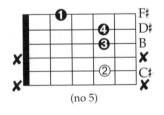

11. Fret

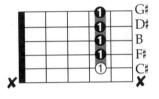

C♯9sus4

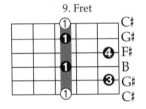

(no 5)

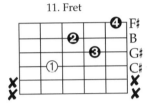

9. Fret

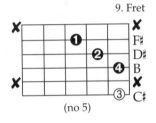

(no 5)

11. Fret

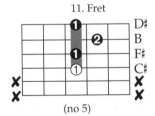

(no 5)

C♯13sus4

4. Fret

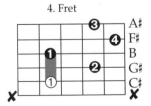

9. Fret

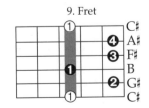

C

C♯/D♭

D

D♯/E♭

E

F

F♯/G♭

G

G♯/A♭

A

A♯/B♭

B

POWER CHORDS

SLASH CHORDS

TRANS-POSING

C♯°

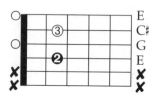

4. Fret

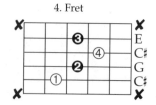

9. Fret

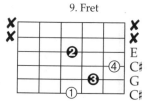

C♯m7♭5

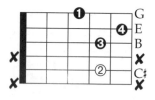

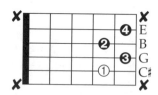

9. Fret

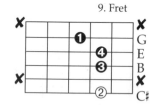

9. Fret

11. Fret

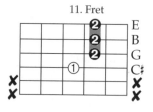

C♯°7

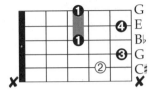

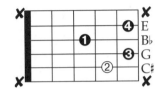

5. Fret

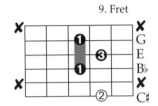

8. Fret

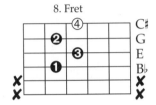

9. Fret

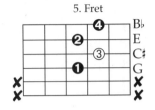

9. Fret

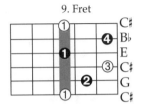

11. Fret

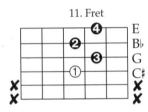

C

C♯/D♭

D

D♯/E♭

E

F

F♯/G♭

G

G♯/A♭

A

A♯/B♭

B

POWER CHORDS

SLASH CHORDS

TRANS-POSING

C♯+

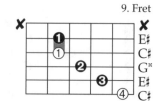

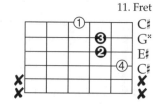

C♯sus4

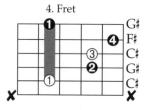

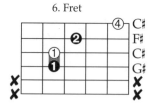

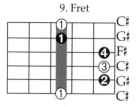

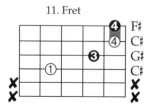

C♯sus2

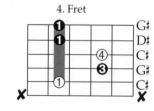

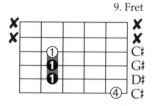

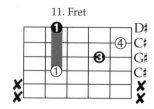

D

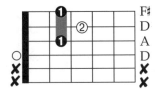

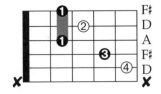

7. Fret

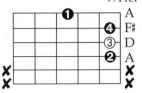

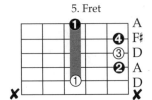

5. Fret

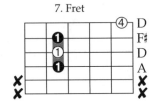

7. Fret

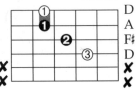

12. Fret

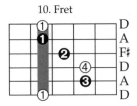

10. Fret

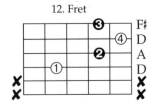

12. Fret

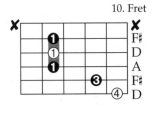

10. Fret

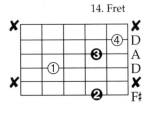

14. Fret

D6

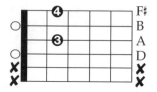
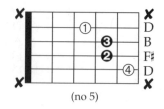
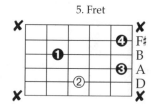

F#
B
A
D

(no 5)

5. Fret

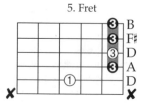
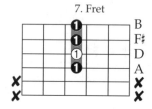
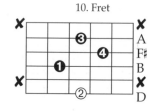

5. Fret

7. Fret

10. Fret

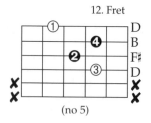
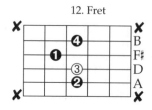

12. Fret

(no 5)

12. Fret

D⁶₉

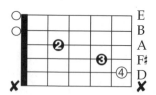
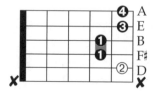
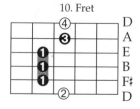

10. Fret

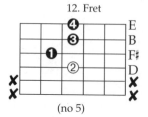

12. Fret

(no 5)

Dmaj7

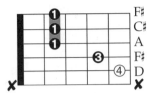

F#
C#
A
F#
D

5. Fret

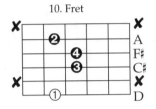

A
F#
C#
A
D

7. Fret

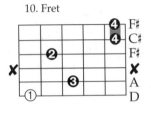

C#
F#
D
A

12. Fret

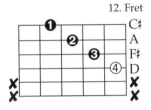

C#
A
F#
D

10. Fret

A
F#
C#
D

10. Fret

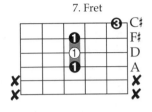

F#
C#
F#
A
D

12. Fret

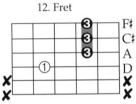

F#
C#
A
D

Dmaj13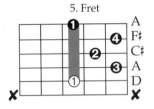

10. Fret

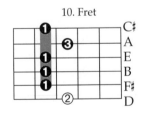

C#
A
E
B
F#
D

10. Fret

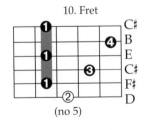

C#
B
E
C#
F#
D

(no 5)

10. Fret

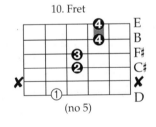

E
B
F#
C#
D

(no 5)

C

C#/Db

D

D#/Eb

E

F

F#/Gb

G

G#/Ab

A

A#/Bb

B

POWER
CHORDS

SLASH
CHORDS

TRANS-
POSING

Dmaj9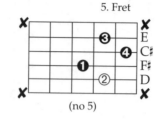

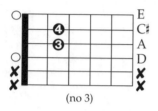

(no 3)

5. Fret
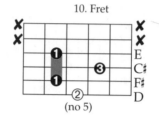

(no 5)

5. Fret
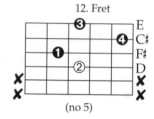

(no 3)

10. Fret
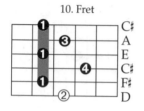

10. Fret
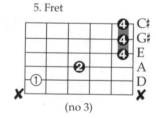

(no 5)

12. Fret
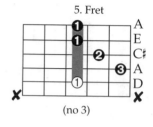

(no 5)

Dmaj9♯11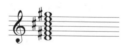

5. Fret
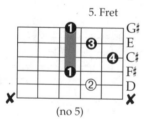

(no 5)

5. Fret

(no 3)

10. Fret
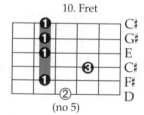

(no 5)

Dmaj7+

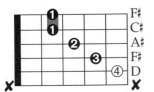

5. Fret

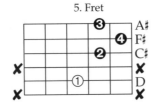

5. Fret

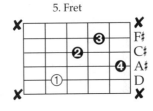

8. Fret

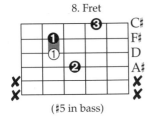

(#5 in bass)

12. Fret

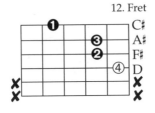

10. Fret

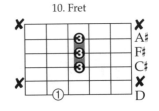

Dmaj7♭5

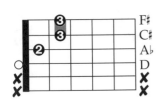

5. Fret

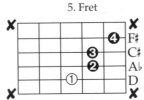

12. Fret

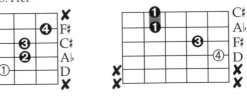

10. Fret

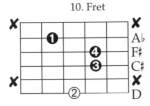

Dmaj13(no9)

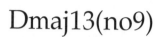

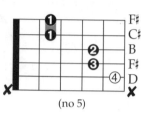

(no 5)

F#
C#
B
F#
D

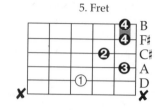

5. Fret

B
F#
C#
A
D

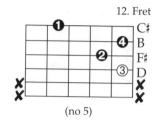

12. Fret

C#
B
F#
D

(no 5)

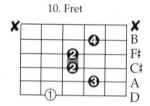

10. Fret

B
F#
C#
A
D

Dadd9

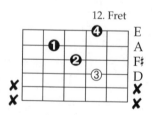

F#
E
A
F#
D

A
E
F#
D

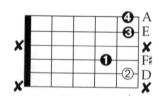

5. Fret

A
F#
E
A
D

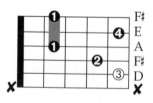

12. Fret

E
A
F#
D

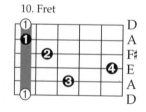

10. Fret

D
A
F#
E
A
D

Dm

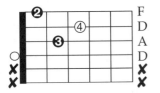

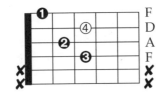

5. Fret

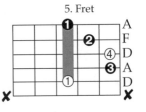

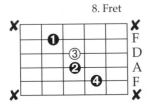

8. Fret

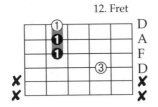

12. Fret

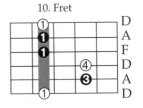

10. Fret

Dm7

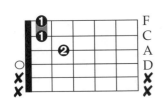

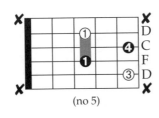

(no 5)

5. Fret

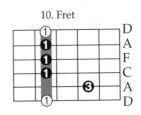

(no 5)

5. Fret

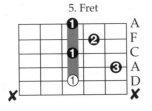

10. Fret

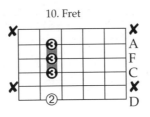

10. Fret

C
C♯/D♭
D
D♯/E♭
E
F
F♯/G♭
G
G♯/A♭
A
A♯/B♭
B
POWER CHORDS
SLASH CHORDS
TRANS- POSING

C

C#/D♭

D

D#/E♭

E

F

F#/G♭

G

G#/A♭

A

A#/B♭

B

POWER CHORDS

SLASH CHORDS

TRANS-POSING

Dm6

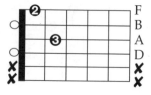
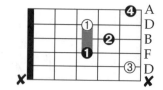
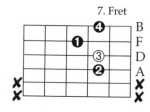

7. Fret

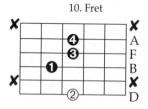
10. Fret
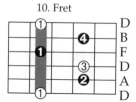
10. Fret

Dm(maj7)

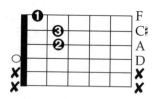
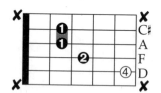
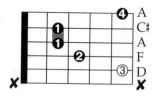

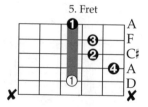
5. Fret
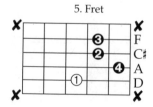
5. Fret
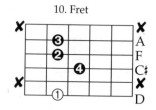
10. Fret

Dm add9

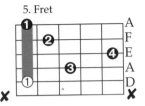

Dm9

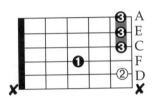

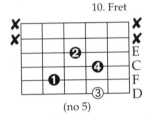

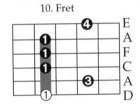

(no 5)

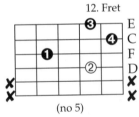

(no 5)

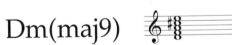

(no 5)

Dm(maj9)

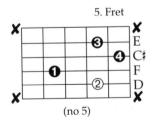

(no 5)

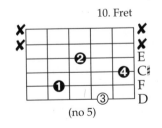

(no 5)

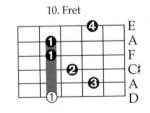

C

C#/Db

D

D#/Eb

E

F

F#/Gb

G

G#/Ab

A

A#/Bb

B

POWER CHORDS

SLASH CHORDS

TRANS- POSING

Dm$^6_9$

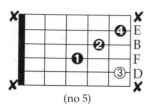

(no 5)

10. Fret

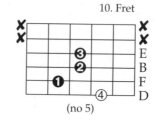

(no 5)

12. Fret

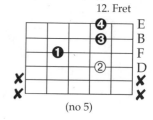

(no 5)

10. Fret

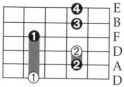

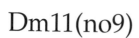

Dm11(no9)

5. Fret

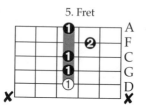

12. Fret

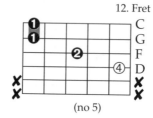

(no 5)

10. Fret

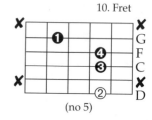

(no 5)

Dm11

10. Fret

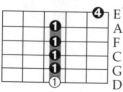

D7

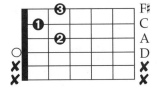
F#
C
A
D

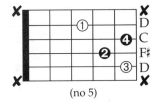
(no 5)
D
C
F#
D

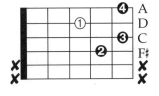
A
D
C
F#

5. Fret
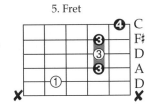
C
F#
D
A
D

5. Fret
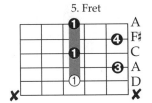
A
F#
C
A
D

7. Fret
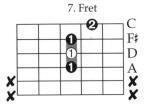
C
F#
D
A

10. Fret
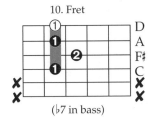
D
A
F#
C

(♭7 in bass)

12. Fret
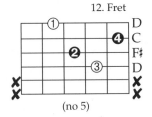
D
C
F#
D

(no 5)

10. Fret
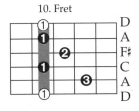
D
A
F#
C
A
D

10. Fret
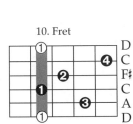
D
C
F#
C
A
D

C
C#/D♭
D
D#/E♭
E
F
F#/G♭
G
G#/A♭
A
A#/B♭
B
POWER CHORDS
SLASH CHORDS
TRANS-POSING

D9

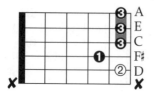

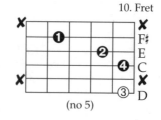
10. Fret
(no 5)

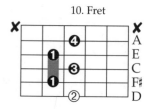
10. Fret

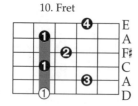
10. Fret

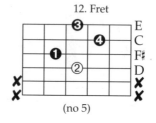
12. Fret
(no 5)

D13

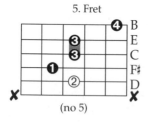
5. Fret
(no 5)

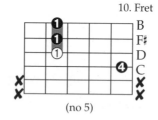
10. Fret
(no 5)

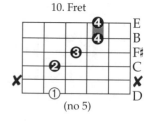
10. Fret
(no 5)

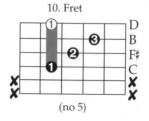
10. Fret
(no 5)

D7♭9

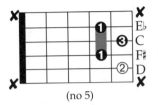

(no 5)   (no 5)   (no 5)

10. Fret

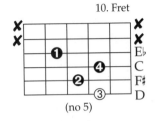

12. Fret

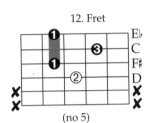

(no 5)

D7♯9

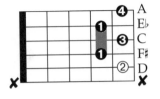

5. Fret   10. Fret   10. Fret

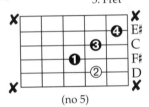   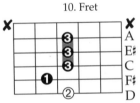   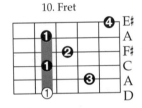

(no 5)

12. Fret

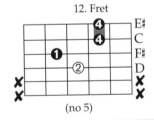

(no 5)

D13♭9

5. Fret   10. Fret

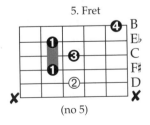   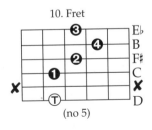

(no 5)   (no 5)

C

C♯/D♭

D

D♯/E♭

E

F

F♯/G♭

G

G♯/A♭

A

A♯/B♭

B

POWER CHORDS

SLASH CHORDS

TRANS-POSING

D7+

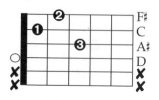

5. Fret

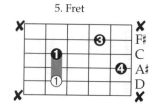

5. Fret

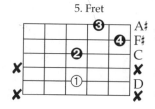

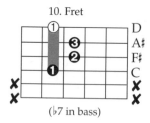

(♭7 in bass)

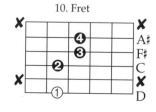

10. Fret

D7♭5

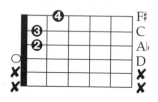

5. Fret

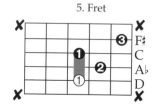

6. Fret

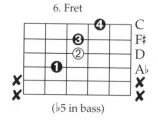

(♭5 in bass)

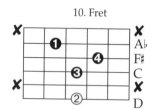

10. Fret

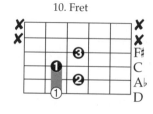

10. Fret

D7 $^{\flat 9}_{\sharp 5}$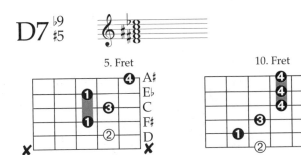

5. Fret   10. Fret

A#   E♭
E♭   A#
C   F#
F#   C
D   F#
                           D

D7 $^{\sharp 9}_{\sharp 5}$

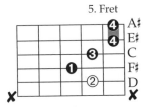
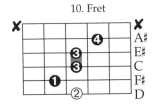

5. Fret   10. Fret

A#   A#
E#   E#
C   C
F#   F#
D   D

D9#11

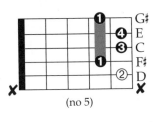
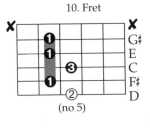

10. Fret

G#   G#
E   E
C   C
F#   F#
D   D

(no 5)   (no 5)

D9+

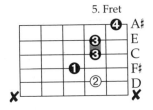
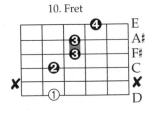

5. Fret   10. Fret

A#   E
E   A#
C   F#
F#   C
D   D

C
C#/D♭
D
D#/E♭
E
F
F#/G♭
G
G#/A♭
A
A#/B♭
B
POWER CHORDS
SLASH CHORDS
TRANS-POSING

C

C#/D♭

D

D#/E♭

E

F

F#/G♭

G

G#/A♭

A

A#/B♭

B

POWER CHORDS

SLASH CHORDS

TRANS-POSING

D7sus4

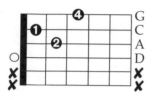

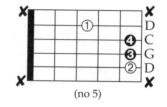

5. Fret

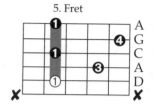

7. Fret

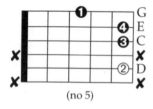

10. Fret

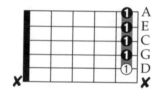

D9sus4

(no 5)

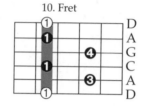

10. Fret

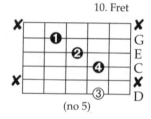

(no 5)

12. Fret

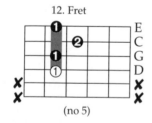

(no 5)

D13sus4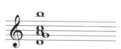

5. Fret

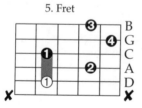

10. Fret

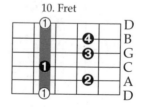

D°

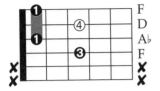

5. Fret

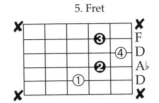

10. Fret

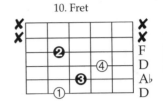

Dm7♭5

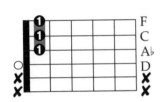

5. Fret

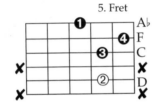

5. Fret

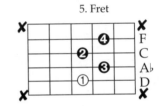

10. Fret

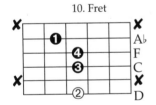

10. Fret

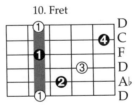

C

C#/D♭

D

D#/E♭

E

F

F#/G♭

G

G#/A♭

A

A#/B♭

B

POWER CHORDS

SLASH CHORDS

TRANS-POSING

D°7

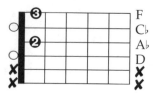

F
C♭
A♭
D

5. Fret

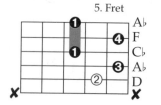

A♭
F
C♭
A♭
D

5. Fret

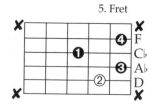

F
C♭
A♭
D

6. Fret

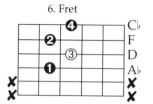

C♭
F
D
A♭

9. Fret

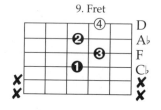

D
A♭
F
C♭

10. Fret

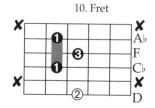

A♭
F
C♭
D

10. Fret

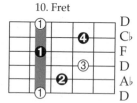

D
C♭
F
D
A♭
D

D+

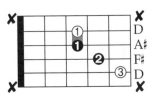

10. Fret

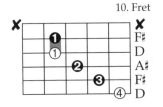

12. Fret

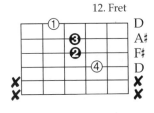

Dsus4

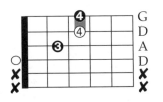

5. Fret

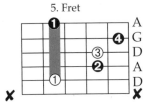

7. Fret

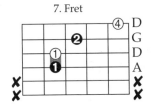

10. Fret

Dsus2

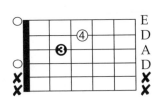

5. Fret

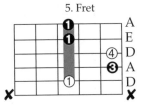

10. Fret

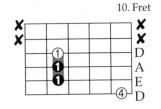

E♭

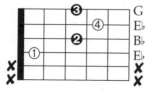

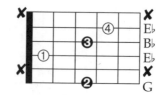

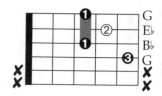

6. Fret

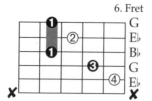

8. Fret

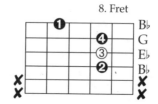

6. Fret

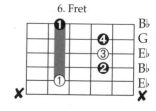

8. Fret

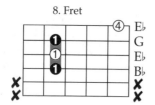

13. Fret

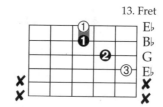

11. Fret

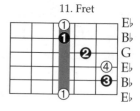

11. Fret

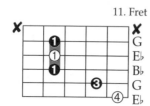

E♭6

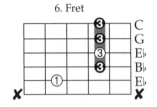
G
C
B♭
E♭

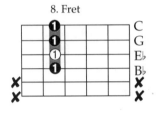
6. Fret
E♭
C
G
E♭
(no 5)

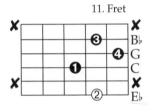
6. Fret
G
C
B♭
E♭

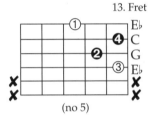
6. Fret
C
G
E♭
B♭
E♭

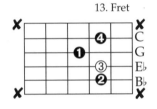
8. Fret
C
G
E♭
B♭

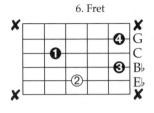
11. Fret
B♭
G
C
E♭

13. Fret
E♭
C
G
E♭
(no 5)

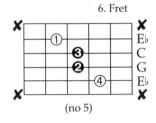
13. Fret
C
G
E♭
B♭

E♭⁶⁄₉

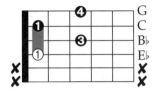

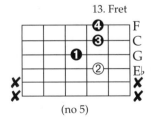
F
C
B♭
G
E♭

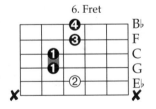
6. Fret
B♭
F
C
G
E♭

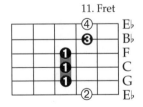
11. Fret
E♭
B♭
F
C
G
E♭

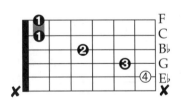
13. Fret
F
C
G
E♭
(no 5)

C
C♯/D♭
D
D♯/E♭
E
F
F♯/G♭
G
G♯/A♭
A
A♯/B♭
B
POWER CHORDS
SLASH CHORDS
TRANS-POSING

E♭maj7

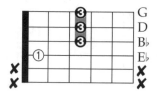

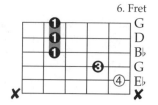

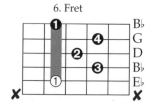

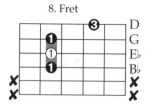

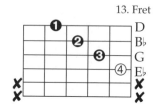

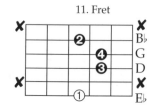

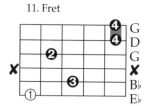

E♭maj13

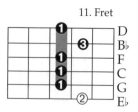

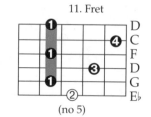

(no 5)

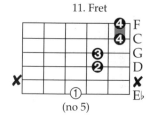

(no 5)

C

C♯/D♭

D

D♯/E♭

E

F

F♯/G♭

G

G♯/A♭

A

A♯/B♭

B

POWER CHORDS

SLASH CHORDS

TRANS-POSING

E♭maj9

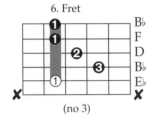

(no 5)

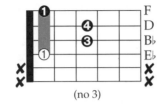

(no 3)

6. Fret

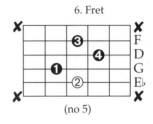

(no 5)

6. Fret

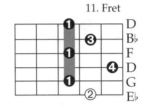

(no 3)

11. Fret

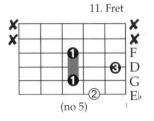

11. Fret

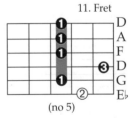

(no 5)

E♭maj9♯11

6. Fret

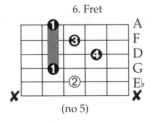

(no 5)

6. Fret

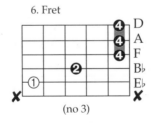

(no 3)

11. Fret

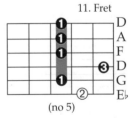

(no 5)

C

C♯/D♭

D

D♯/E♭

E

F

F♯/G♭

G

G♯/A♭

A

A♯/B♭

B

POWER CHORDS

SLASH CHORDS

TRANS- POSING

E♭maj7+

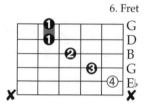
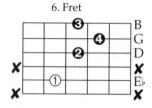
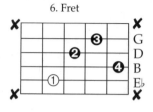

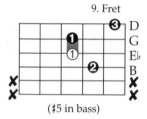
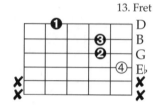
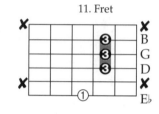

(♯5 in bass)

E♭maj7♭5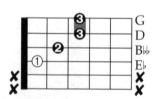

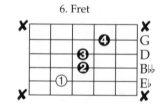
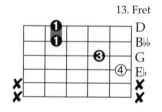

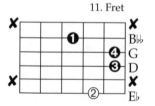

E♭maj13(no9)

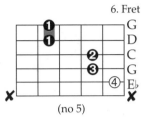

6. Fret — G D C G E♭ (no 5)

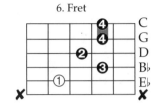

6. Fret — C G D B♭ E♭

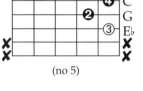

13. Fret — D C G E♭ (no 5)

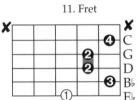

11. Fret — C G D B♭ E♭

E♭add9

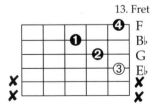

6. Fret — G F B♭ G E♭

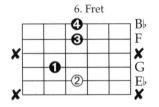

6. Fret — B♭ F G E♭

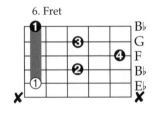

6. Fret — B♭ G F B♭ E♭

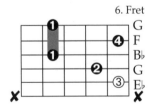

13. Fret — F B♭ G E♭

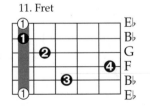

11. Fret — E♭ B♭ G F B♭ E♭

C

C♯/D♭

D

D♯/E♭

E

F

F♯/G♭

G

G♯/A♭

A

A♯/B♭

B

POWER CHORDS

SLASH CHORDS

TRANS-POSING

E♭m

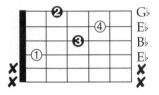

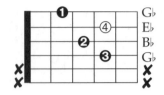

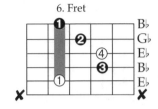

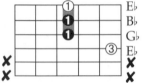

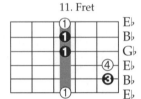

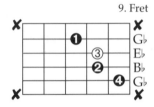

E♭m7

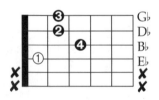

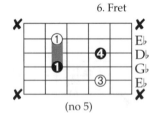

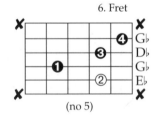

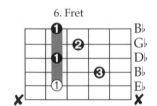

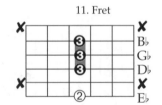

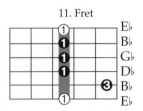

E♭m6

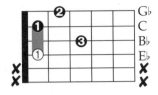

6. Fret

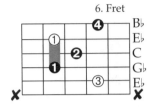

8. Fret

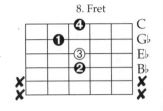

11. Fret

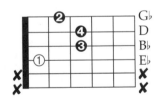

11. Fret

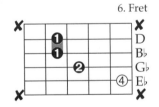

E♭m(maj7)

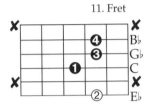

6. Fret

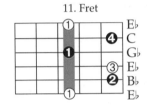

6. Fret

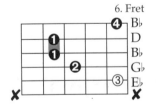

6. Fret

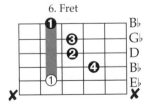

6. Fret

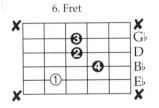

11. Fret

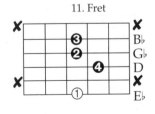

C
C♯/D♭
D
D♯/E♭
E
F
F♯/G♭
G
G♯/A♭
A
A♯/B♭
B
POWER CHORDS
SLASH CHORDS
TRANS- POSING

E♭m add9

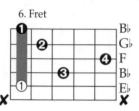
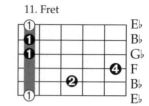
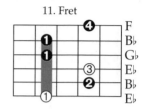

E♭m9

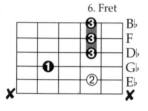
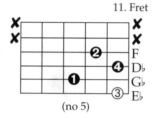
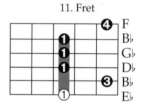

(no 5)

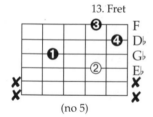

(no 5)

E♭m(maj9)

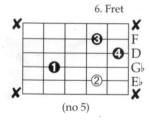

(no 5)

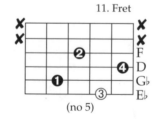

(no 5)

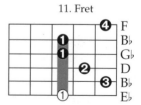

C
C#/D♭
D
D#/E♭
E
F
F#/G♭
G
G#/A♭
A
A#/B♭
B
POWER CHORDS
SLASH CHORDS
TRANS-POSING

E♭m$^6_9$

6. Fret

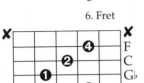

(no 5)

11. Fret

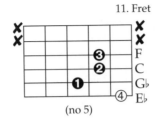

(no 5)

13. Fret

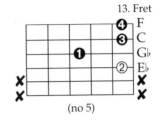

(no 5)

11. Fret

E♭m11(no9)

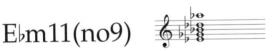

6. Fret

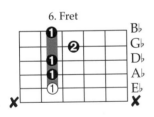

13. Fret

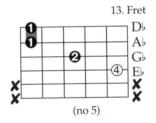

(no 5)

11. Fret

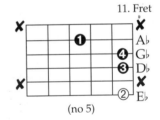

(no 5)

E♭m11

11. Fret

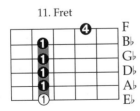

C

C♯/D♭

D

D♯/E♭

E

F

F♯/G♭

G

G♯/A♭

A

A♯/B♭

B

POWER CHORDS

SLASH CHORDS

TRANS-POSING

E♭7

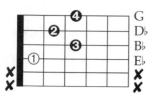
G
D♭
B♭
E♭

6. Fret

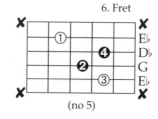
E♭
D♭
G
E♭

(no 5)

5. Fret

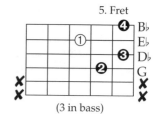
B♭
E♭
D♭
G

(3 in bass)

6. Fret

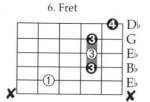
D♭
G
E♭
B♭
E♭

6. Fret

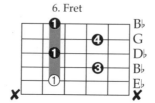
B♭
G
D♭
B♭
E♭

8. Fret

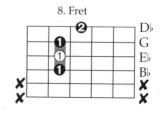
D♭
G
E♭
B♭

11. Fret

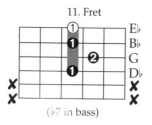
E♭
B♭
G
D♭

(♭7 in bass)

13. Fret

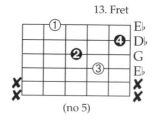
E♭
D♭
G
E♭

(no 5)

11. Fret

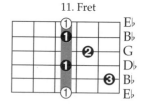
E♭
B♭
G
D♭
B♭
E♭

11. Fret

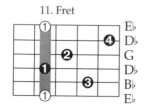
E♭
D♭
G
D♭
B♭
E♭

E♭9

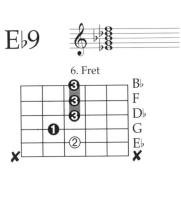

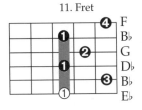
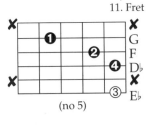
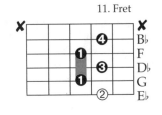

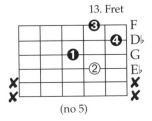

E♭13

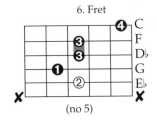
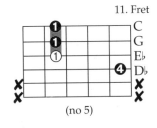
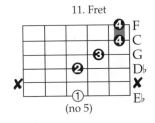

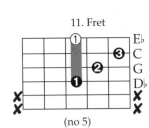

E♭7♭9

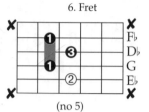

6. Fret

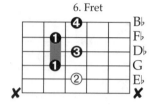

6. Fret

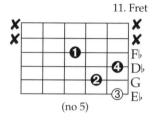

11. Fret

(no 5)

(no 5)

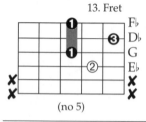

13. Fret

(no 5)

E♭7♯9

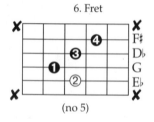

6. Fret

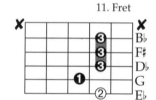

11. Fret

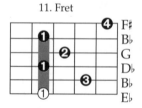

11. Fret

(no 5)

13. Fret

(no 5)

E♭13♭9

6. Fret

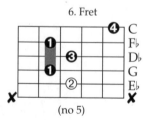

11. Fret

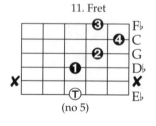

(no 5)

(no 5)

E♭7+

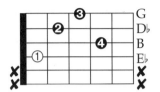

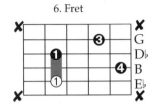
6. Fret

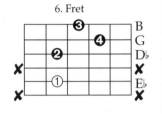
6. Fret

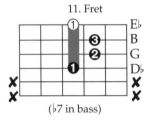
11. Fret
(♭7 in bass)

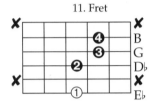
11. Fret

E♭7♭5

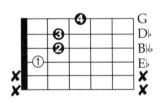

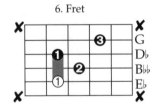
6. Fret

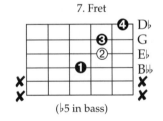
7. Fret
(♭5 in bass)

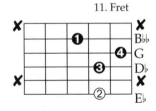
11. Fret

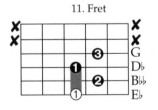
11. Fret

C

C♯/D♭

D

D♯/E♭

E

F

F♯/G♭

G

G♯/A♭

A

A♯/B♭

B

POWER CHORDS

SLASH CHORDS

TRANS-POSING

E♭7 $^{♭9}_{♯5}$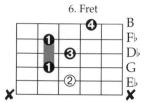

6. Fret

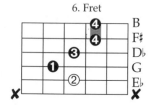

11. Fret

E♭7 $^{♯9}_{♯5}$

6. Fret

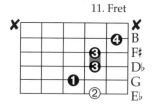

11. Fret

E♭9♯11

6. Fret

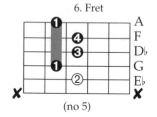

(no 5)

11. Fret

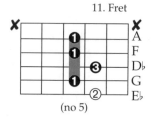

(no 5)

E♭9+

6. Fret

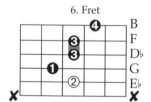

11. Fret

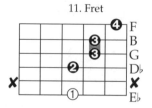

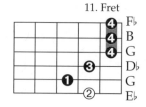

E♭7sus4

A♭
D♭
B♭
E♭

6. Fret
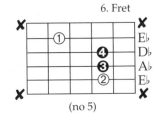
E♭
D♭
A♭
E♭
(no 5)

6. Fret
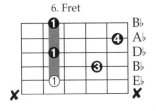
B♭
A♭
D♭
B♭
E♭

8. Fret
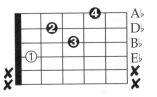
D♭
A♭
E♭
B♭

11. Fret
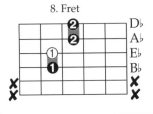
E♭
B♭
A♭
D♭
B♭
E♭

E♭9sus4

F
D♭
A♭
E♭
(no 5)

6. Fret
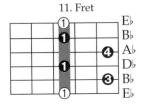
A♭
F
D♭
E♭
(no 5)

6. Fret
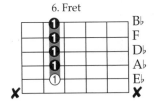
B♭
F
D♭
A♭
E♭

11. Fret
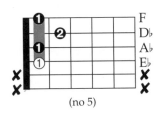
A♭
F
D♭
E♭
(no 5)

E♭13sus4

6. Fret
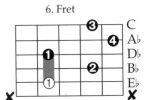
C
A♭
D♭
B♭
E♭

11. Fret
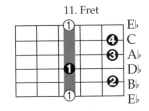
E♭
C
A♭
D♭
B♭
E♭

C
C♯/D♭
D
D♯/E♭
E
F
F♯/G♭
G
G♯/A♭
A
A♯/B♭
B
POWER CHORDS
SLASH CHORDS
TRANS- POSING

E♭°

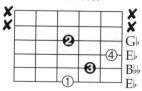

6. Fret

11. Fret

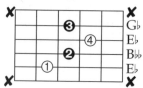

E♭m7♭5

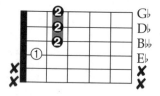

6. Fret

6. Fret

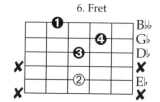

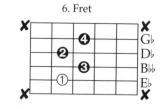

11. Fret

11. Fret

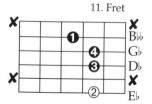

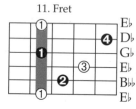

E♭°7

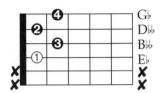

6. Fret

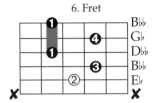

6. Fret

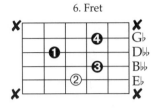

7. Fret

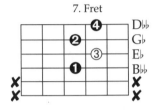

10. Fret

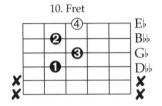

11. Fret

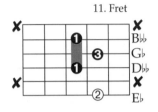

11. Fret

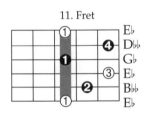

C

C♯/D♭

D

D♯/E♭

E

F

F♯/G♭

G

G♯/A♭

A

A♯/B♭

B

POWER CHORDS

SLASH CHORDS

TRANS-POSING

E♭+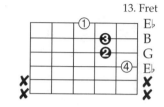

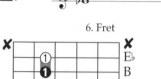

6. Fret	11. Fret	13. Fret

E♭sus4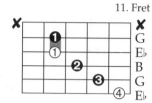

	6. Fret	8. Fret

11. Fret

E♭sus2

	6. Fret	11. Fret

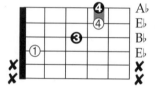

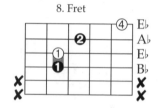
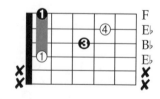

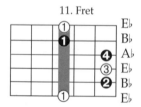

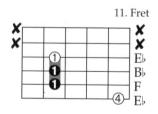
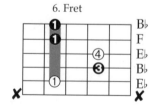
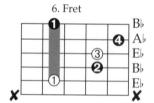

E

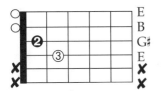
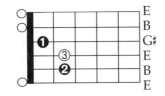
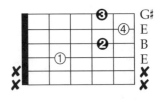

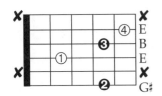
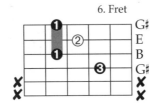
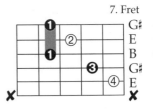

6. Fret   7. Fret

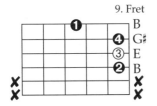
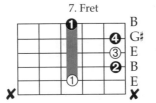
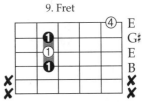

9. Fret   7. Fret   9. Fret

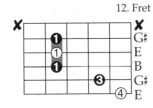

12. Fret

C
C#/Db
D
D#/Eb
E
F
F#/Gb
G
G#/Ab
A
A#/Bb
B
POWER CHORDS
SLASH CHORDS
TRANS- POSING

E6

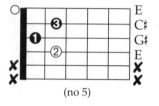

E
C#
G#
E
(no 5)

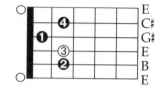

E
C#
G#
E
B
E

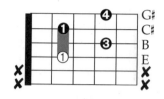

G#
C#
B
E

7. Fret

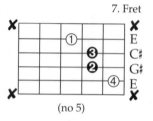

E
C#
G#
E
(no 5)

7. Fret

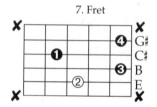

G#
C#
B
E

7. Fret

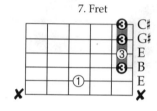

C#
G#
E
B
E

9. Fret

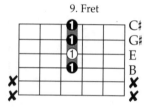

C#
G#
E
B

12. Fret

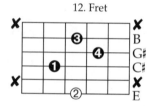

B
G#
C#
E

E $^6_9$

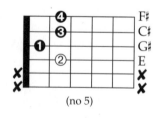

F#
C#
G#
E
(no 5)

2. Fret

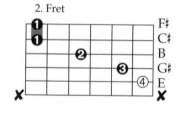

F#
C#
B
G#
E

7. Fret

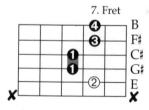

B
F#
C#
G#
E

12. Fret

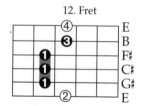

E
B
F#
C#
G#
E

Emaj7

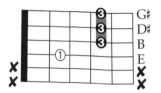
G#
D#
B
E

7. Fret
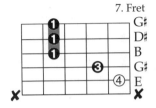
G#
D#
B
G#
E

7. Fret
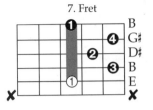
B
G#
D#
B
E

9. Fret
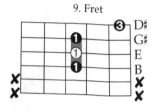
D#
G#
E
B

14. Fret
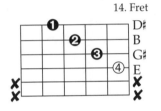
D#
B
G#
E

12. Fret
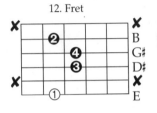
B
G#
D#
E

12. Fret
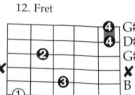
G#
D#
G#
B
E

Emaj13

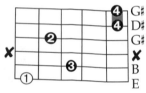

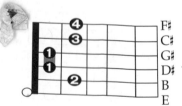
F#
C#
G#
D#
B
E

12. Fret
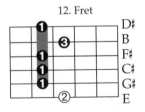
D#
B
F#
C#
G#
E

12. Fret
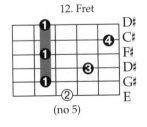
D#
C#
F#
D#
G#
E
(no 5)

C
C#/Db
D
D#/Eb
E
F
F#/Gb
G
G#/Ab
A
A#/Bb
B
POWER CHORDS
SLASH CHORDS
TRANS- POSING

Emaj9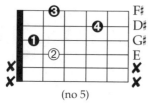

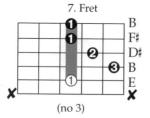

(no 5)

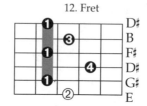

F#
D#
G#
B
E

(no 3)

7. Fret

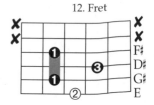

F#
D#
G#
E

(no 5)

7. Fret

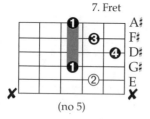

B
F#
D#
B
E

(no 3)

12. Fret

D#
B
F#
D#
G#
E

12. Fret

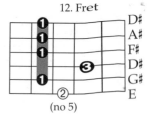

F#
D#
G#
E

(no 5)

Emaj9#11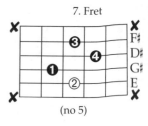

7. Fret

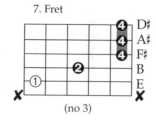

A#
F#
D#
G#
E

(no 5)

7. Fret

D#
A#
F#
B
E

(no 3)

12. Fret

D#
A#
F#
D#
G#
E

(no 5)

C
C#/Db
D
D#/Eb
E
F
F#/Gb
G
G#/Ab
A
A#/Bb
B
POWER CHORDS
SLASH CHORDS
TRANS-POSING

Emaj7+

7. Fret
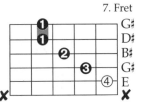
G#
D#
B#
G#
E

7. Fret
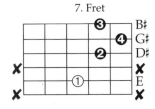
B#
G#
D#
E

7. Fret
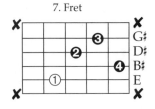
G#
D#
B#
E

10. Fret
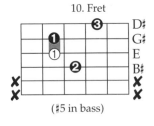
D#
G#
E
B#

(#5 in bass)

14. Fret
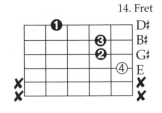
D#
B#
G#
E

12. Fret
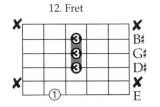
B#
G#
D#
E

Emaj7♭5

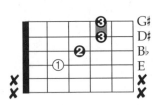
G#
D#
B♭
E

7. Fret
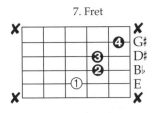
G#
D#
B♭
E

14. Fret
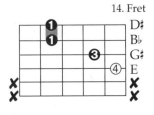
D#
B♭
G#
E

12. Fret
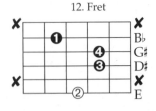
B♭
G#
D#
E

C
C#/D♭
D
D#/E♭
E
F
F#/G♭
G
G#/A♭
A
A#/B♭
B
POWER CHORDS
SLASH CHORDS
TRANS-POSING

Emaj13(no9)

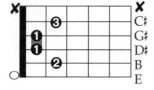

7. Fret
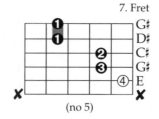
(no 5)

7. Fret
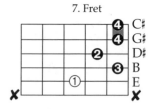

14. Fret
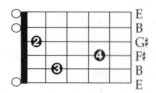
(no 5)

Eadd9

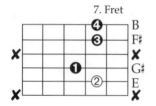

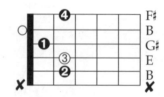

7. Fret
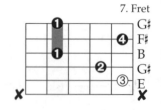

7. Fret
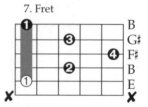

7. Fret

Em

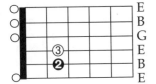

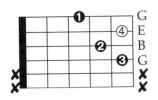

Em7

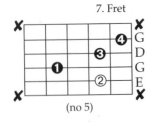

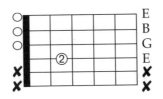

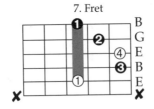

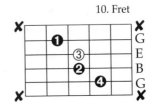

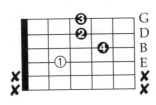

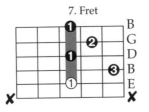

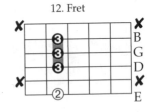

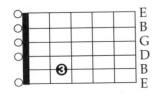

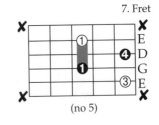

C

C#/Db

D

D#/Eb

E

F

F#/Gb

G

G#/Ab

A

A#/Bb

B

POWER CHORDS

SLASH CHORDS

TRANS-POSING

Em6

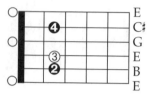

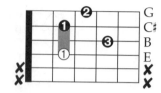

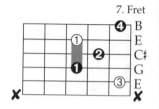
7. Fret

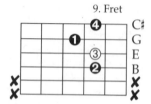
9. Fret

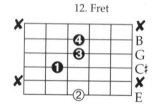
12. Fret

Em(maj7)

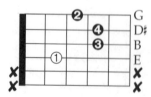

7. Fret

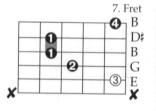
7. Fret

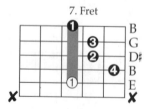
7. Fret

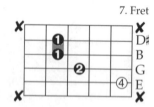
7. Fret

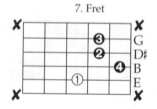
12. Fret

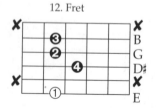

C
C♯/D♭
D
D♯/E♭
E
F
F♯/G♭
G
G♯/A♭
A
A♯/B♭
B
POWER CHORDS
SLASH CHORDS
TRANS- POSING

Em add9

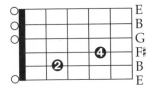
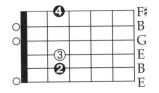

7. Fret
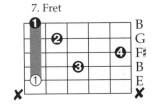

Em9

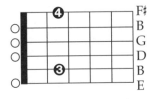

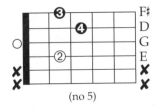
(no 5)

7. Fret
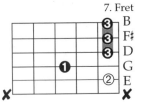

12. Fret
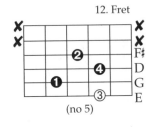
(no 5)

Em(maj9)

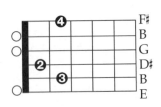

7. Fret
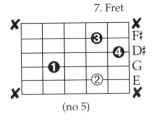
(no 5)

12. Fret
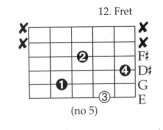
(no 5)

C

C#/Db

D

D#/Eb

E

F

F#/Gb

G

G#/Ab

A

A#/Bb

B

POWER
CHORDS

SLASH
CHORDS

TRANS-
POSING

Em $^6_9$

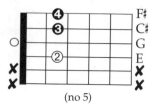

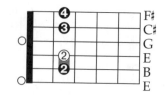

7. Fret

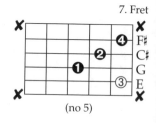

(no 5)

(no 5)

12. Fret

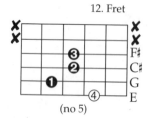

(no 5)

Em11(no9)

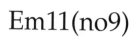 

7. Fret

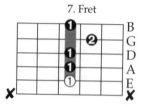

14. Fret

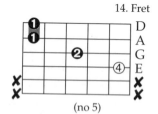

(no 5)

12. Fret

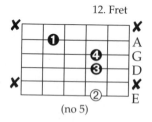

(no 5)

Em11

12. Fret

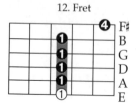

C

C♯/D♭

D

D♯/E♭

E

F

F♯/G♭

G

G♯/A♭

A

A♯/B♭

B

POWER CHORDS

SLASH CHORDS

TRANS-POSING

E7

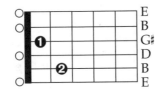

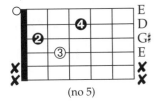
(no 5)

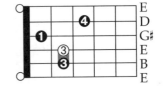

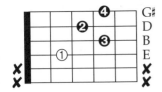

6. Fret

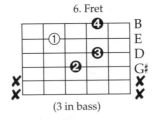
(3 in bass)

7. Fret

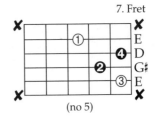
(no 5)

7. Fret

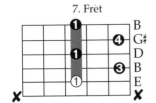

7. Fret

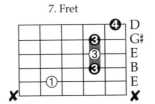

9. Fret

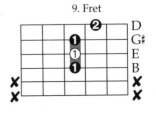

12. Fret

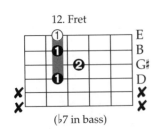
(♭7 in bass)

C
C♯/D♭
D
D♯/E♭
E
F
F♯/G♭
G
G♯/A♭
A
A♯/B♭
B
POWER CHORDS
SLASH CHORDS
TRANS- POSING

E9

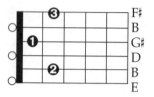

F#
B
G#
D
B
E

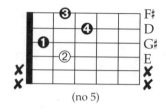

F#
D
G#
E

(no 5)

7. Fret

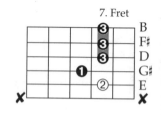

B
F#
D
G#
E

12. Fret

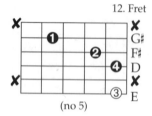

G#
F#
D
E

(no 5)

12. Fret

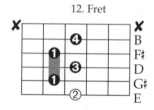

B
F#
D
G#
E

E13

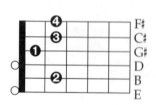

F#
C#
G#
D
B
E

7. Fret

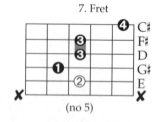

C#
F#
D
G#
E

(no 5)

12. Fret

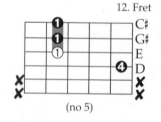

C#
G#
E
D

(no 5)

12. Fret

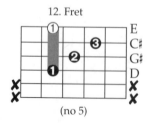

E
C#
G#
D

(no 5)

E7♭9

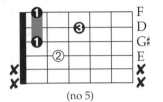

(no 5)

F
D
G#
E

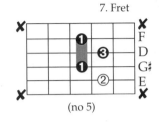

7. Fret

(no 5)

F
D
G#
E

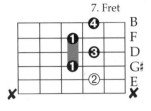

7. Fret

B
F
D
G#
E

12. Fret

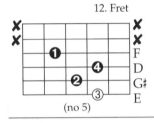

(no 5)

F
D
G#
E

E7#9

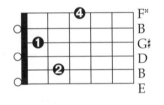

F*
B
G#
D
B
E

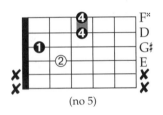

F*
D
G#
E

(no 5)

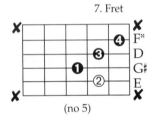

7. Fret

F*
D
G#
E

(no 5)

12. Fret

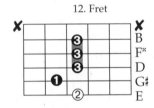

B
F*
D
G#
E

E13♭9

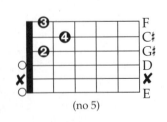

F
C#
G#
D
E

(no 5)

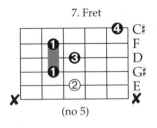

7. Fret

C#
F
D
G#
E

(no 5)

C

C#/D♭

D

D#/E♭

E

F

F#/G♭

G

G#/A♭

A

A#/B♭

B

POWER CHORDS

SLASH CHORDS

TRANS- POSING

E7+

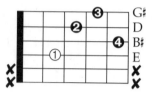

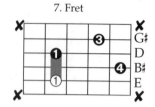
7. Fret

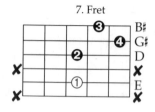
7. Fret

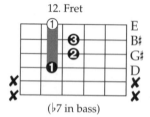
12. Fret

(♭7 in bass)

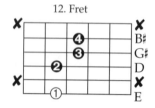
12. Fret

E7♭5

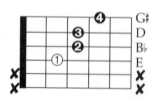

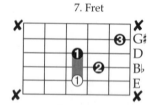
7. Fret

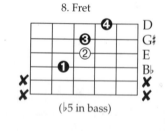
8. Fret

(♭5 in bass)

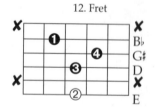
12. Fret

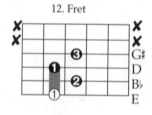
12. Fret

E7 $^{\flat 9}_{\sharp 5}$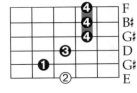

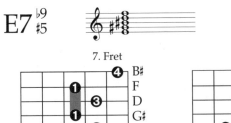

7. Fret — B♯ F D G♯ E

12. Fret — F B♯ G♯ D G♯ E

E7 $^{\sharp 9}_{\sharp 5}$

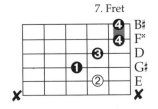 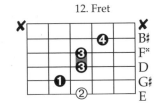

7. Fret — B♯ F× D G♯ E

12. Fret — B♯ F× D G♯ E

E9♯11

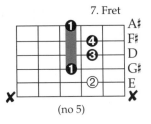 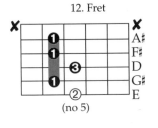

7. Fret — A♯ F♯ D G♯ E
(no 5)

12. Fret — A♯ F♯ D G♯ E
(no 5)

E9+

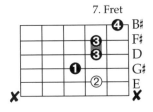 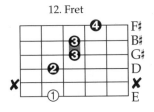

7. Fret — B♯ F♯ D G♯ E

12. Fret — F♯ B♯ G♯ D E

C

C♯/D♭

D

D♯/E♭

E

F

F♯/G♭

G

G♯/A♭

A

A♯/B♭

B

POWER CHORDS

SLASH CHORDS

TRANS- POSING

E7sus4

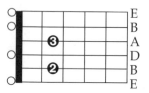
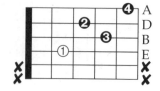
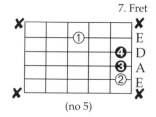

(no 5)

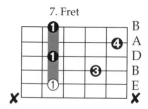
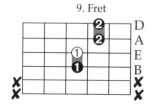

E9sus4

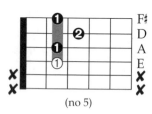
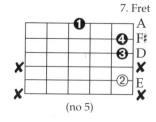
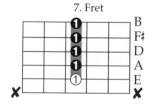

(no 5)   (no 5)

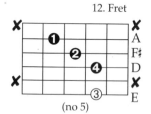

(no 5)

E13sus4

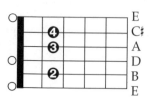
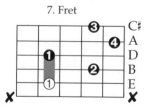

E°

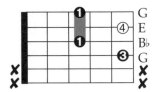

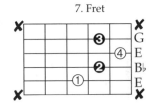

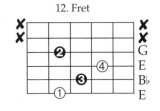

Em7♭5

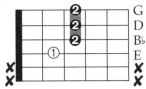

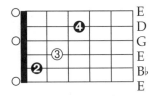

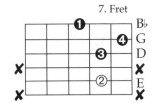

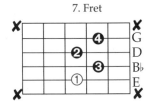

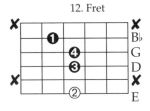

E°7

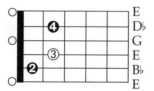

E
D♭
G
E
B♭
E

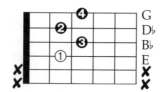

G
D♭
B♭
E

7. Fret

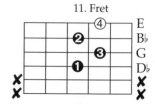

B♭
G
D♭
B♭
E

7. Fret

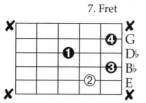

G
D♭
B♭
E

8. Fret

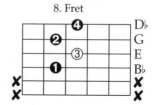

D♭
G
E
B♭

11. Fret

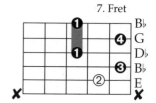

E
B♭
G
D♭

12. Fret

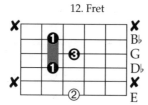

B♭
G
D♭
E

E+

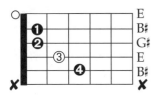 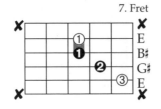 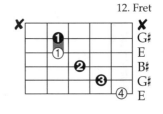

Esus4

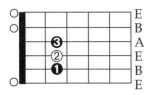 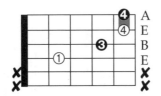 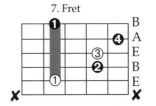

Esus2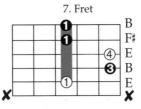

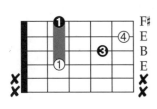 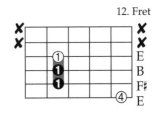

C
C♯/D♭
D
D♯/E♭
E
F
F♯/G♭
G
G♯/A♭
A
A♯/B♭
B
POWER CHORDS
SLASH CHORDS
TRANS- POSING

F

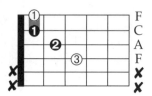
F
C
A
F

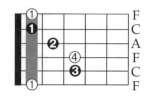
F
C
A
F
C
F

3. Fret

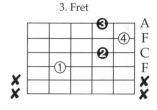
A
F
C
F

5. Fret

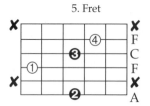
F
C
F
A

7. Fret

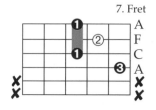
A
F
C
A

8. Fret

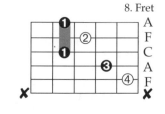
A
F
C
A
F

10. Fret

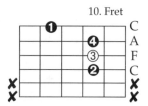
C
A
F
C

8. Fret

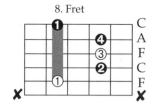
C
A
F
C
F

10. Fret

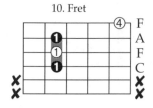
F
A
F
C

13. Fret

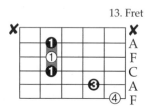
A
F
C
A
F

F6

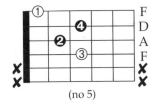
(no 5)

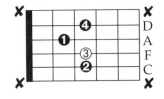

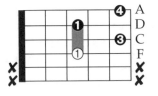

8. Fret
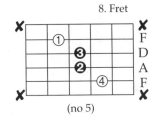
(no 5)

8. Fret
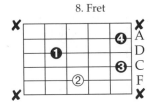

8. Fret
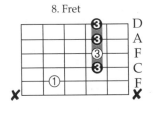

10. Fret
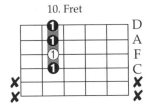

11. Fret
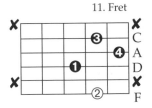

F $^6_9$

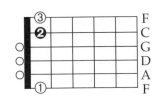

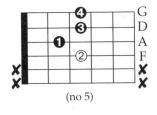
(no 5)

8. Fret
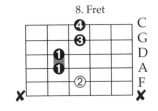

8. Fret
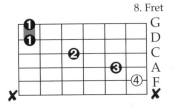

C
C♯/D♭
D
D♯/E♭
E
F
F♯/G♭
G
G♯/A♭
A
A♯/B♭
B
POWER CHORDS
SLASH CHORDS
TRANS-POSING

Fmaj7

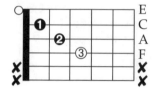
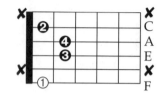
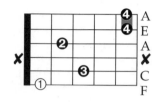

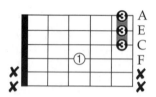
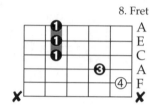
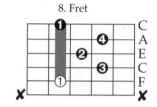

8. Fret 8. Fret

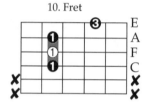

10. Fret

Fmaj13

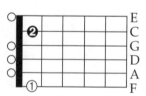
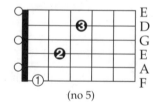
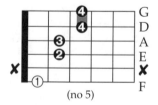

(no 5) (no 5)

Fmaj9

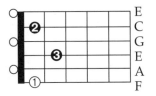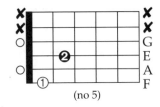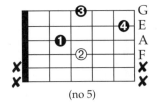

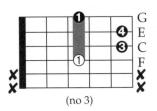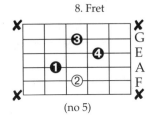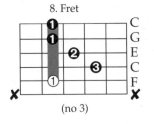

Fmaj9#11

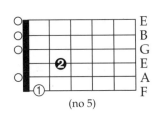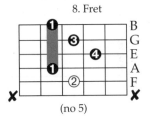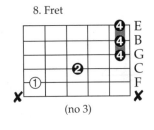

C

C#/Db

D

D#/Eb

E

F

F#/Gb

G

G#/Ab

A

A#/Bb

B

POWER CHORDS

SLASH CHORDS

TRANS-POSING

Fmaj7+

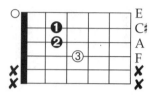
E
C#
A
F

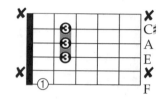
C#
A
E
F

8. Fret

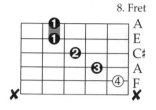
A
E
C#
A
F

8. Fret

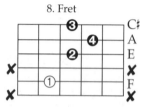
C#
A
E
F

8. Fret

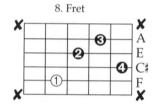
A
E
C#
F

11. Fret

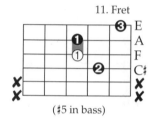
E
A
F
C#

(#5 in bass)

Fmaj7♭5

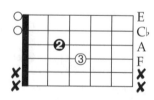
E
C♭
A
F

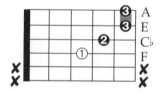
A
E
C♭
F

8. Fret

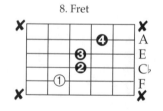
A
E
C♭
F

13. Fret

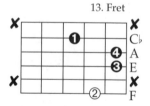
C♭
A
E
F

Fmaj13(no9)

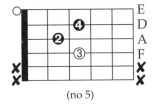

(no 5)

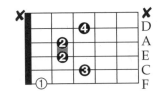

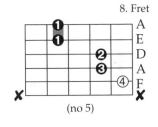

8. Fret

(no 5)

8. Fret

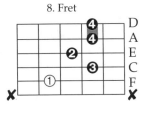

Fadd9

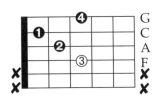

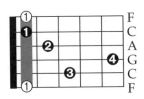

8. Fret

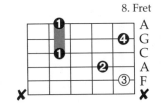

8. Fret

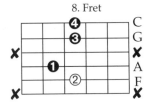

8. Fret

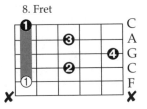

C
C♯/D♭
D
D♯/E♭
E
F
F♯/G♭
G
G♯/A♭
A
A♯/B♭
B
POWER CHORDS
SLASH CHORDS
TRANS-POSING

Fm

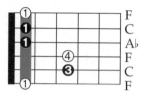

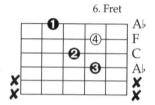 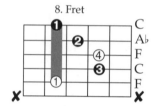 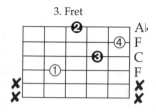

3. Fret

6. Fret   8. Fret   11. Fret

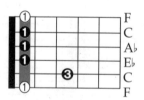 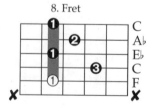 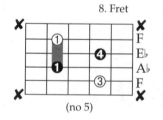

Fm7

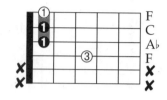

8. Fret

(no 5)

8. Fret   8. Fret   13. Fret

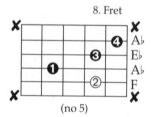 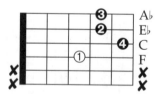 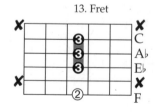

(no 5)

C
C♯/D♭
D
D♯/E♭
E
F
F♯/G♭
G
G♯/A♭
A
A♯/B♭
B
POWER CHORDS
SLASH CHORDS
TRANS-POSING

Fm6

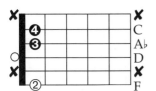
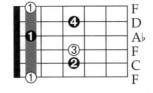
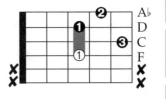

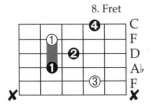
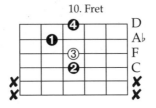

8. Fret   10. Fret

Fm(maj7)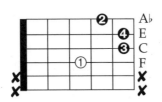

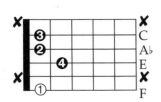
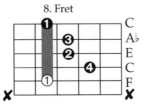
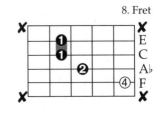

8. Fret

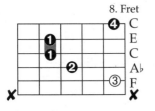
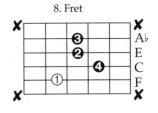

8. Fret   8. Fret   8. Fret

C
C#/Db
D
D#/Eb
E
F
F#/Gb
G
G#/Ab
A
A#/Bb
B
POWER CHORDS
SLASH CHORDS
TRANS-POSING

Fm add9

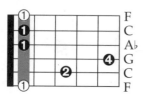

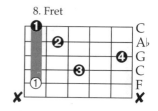

Fm9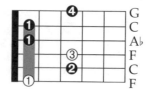

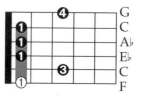

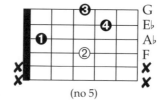

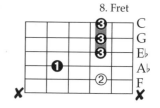

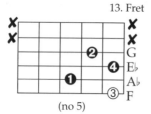

Fm(maj9)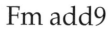

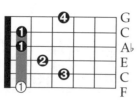

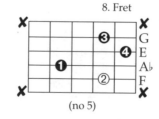

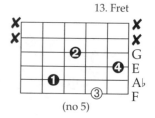

Fm $^6_9$

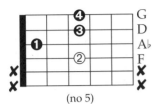   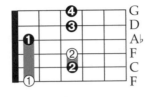   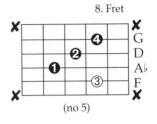

8. Fret

(no 5)   (no 5)

13. Fret

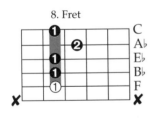

(no 5)

Fm11(no9)

8. Fret   15. Fret   13. Fret

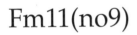   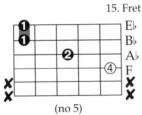   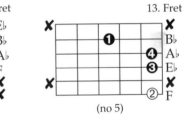

(no 5)   (no 5)

Fm11

13. Fret

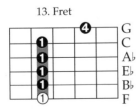

C
C#/Db
D
D#/Eb
E
F
F#/Gb
G
G#/Ab
A
A#/Bb
B
POWER CHORDS
SLASH CHORDS
TRANS-POSING

F7

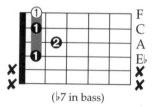
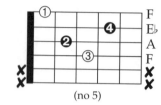
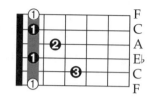

(♭7 in bass) (no 5)

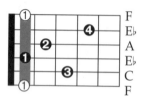
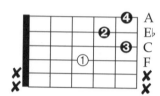
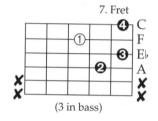

7. Fret

(3 in bass)

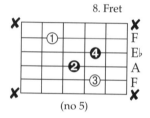
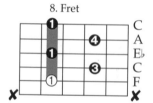
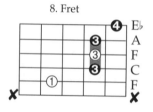

8. Fret 8. Fret 8. Fret

(no 5)

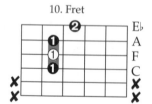

10. Fret

F9

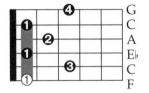

G
C
A
E♭
C
F

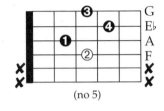

G
E♭
A
F

(no 5)

8. Fret

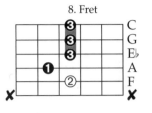

C
G
E♭
A
F

13. Fret

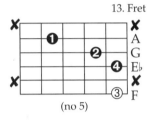

A
G
E♭
F

(no 5)

13. Fret

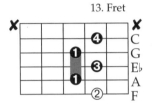

C
G
E♭
A
F

F13

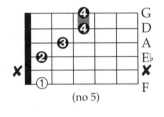

G
D
A
E♭
F

(no 5)

8. Fret

D
G
E♭
A
F

(no 5)

13. Fret

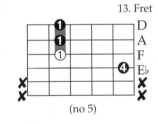

D
A
F
E♭

(no 5)

13. Fret

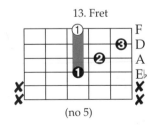

F
D
A
E♭

(no 5)

C
C♯/D♭
D
D♯/E♭
E
F
F♯/G♭
G
G♯/A♭
A
A♯/B♭
B
POWER CHORDS
SLASH CHORDS
TRANS-POSING

F7♭9

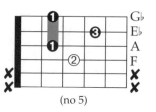
(no 5)

8. Fret

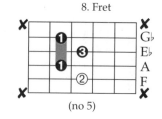
(no 5)

8. Fret

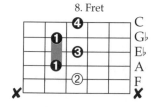

13. Fret

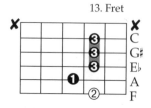
(no 5)

F7♯9

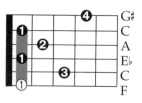

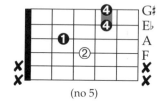
(no 5)

8. Fret

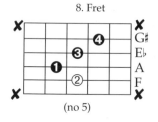
(no 5)

13. Fret

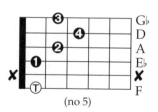

F13♭9

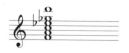

(no 5)

8. Fret

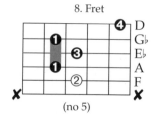
(no 5)

F7+

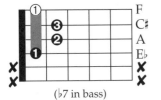

(♭7 in bass)

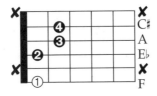

3. Fret

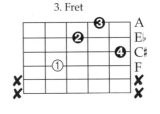

8. Fret

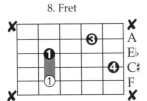

8. Fret

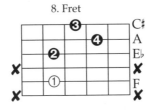

F7♭5

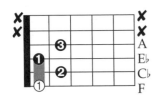

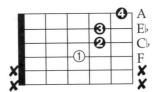

8. Fret

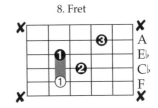

9. Fret

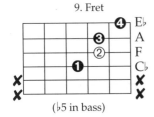

(♭5 in bass)

13. Fret

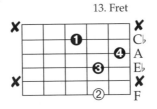

C

C♯/D♭

D

D♯/E♭

E

F

F♯/G♭

G

G♯/A♭

A

A♯/B♭

B

POWER CHORDS

SLASH CHORDS

TRANS-POSING

F7 $^{\flat 9}_{\sharp 5}$

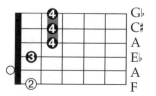

8. Fret

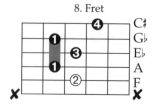

F7 $^{\sharp 9}_{\sharp 5}$

8. Fret   13. Fret

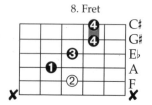   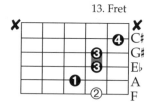

F9♯11

8. Fret   13. Fret

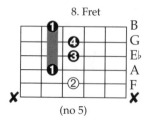   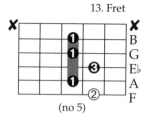

(no 5)   (no 5)

F9+

8. Fret

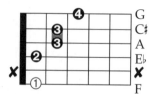

F7sus4

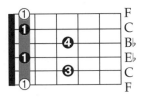

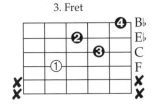
3. Fret
8. Fret

(no 5)

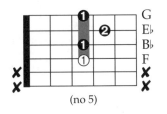
8. Fret

10. Fret

F9sus4

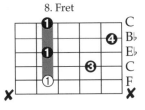
(no 5)

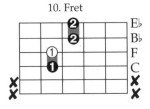
8. Fret
(no 5)

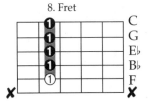
8. Fret

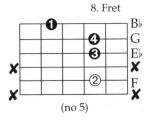
13. Fret
(no 5)

F13sus4

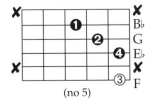

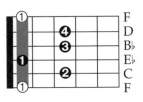

8. Fret

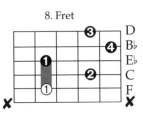

C
C#/Db
D
D#/Eb
E
F
F#/Gb
G
G#/Ab
A
A#/Bb
B
POWER CHORDS
SLASH CHORDS
TRANS- POSING

F°

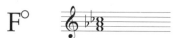

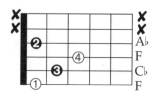

6. Fret

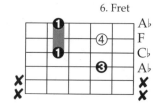

Ab
F
Cb
Ab

8. Fret

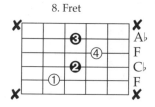

Ab
F
Cb
F

Fm7b5

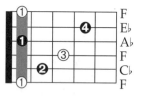

F
Eb
Ab
F
Cb
F

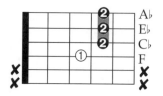

Ab
Eb
Cb
F

8. Fret

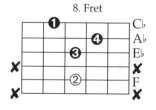

Cb
Ab
Eb
F

8. Fret

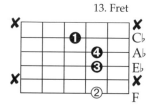

Ab
Eb
Cb
F

13. Fret

Cb
Ab
Eb
F

F°7

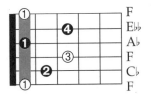

F
E♭♭
A♭
F
C♭
F

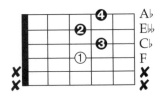

A♭
E♭♭
C♭
F

8. Fret

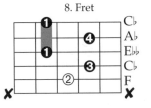

C♭
A♭
E♭♭
C♭
F

8. Fret

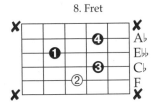

A♭
E♭♭
C♭
F

9. Fret

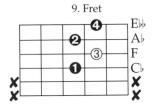

E♭♭
A♭
F
C♭

12. Fret

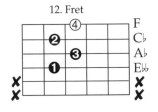

F
C♭
A♭
E♭♭

13. Fret

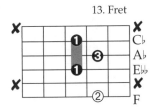

C♭
A♭
E♭♭
F

C

C♯/D♭

D

D♯/E♭

E

F

F♯/G♭

G

G♯/A♭

A

A♯/B♭

B

POWER
CHORDS

SLASH
CHORDS

TRANS-
POSING

F+

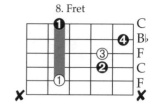

8. Fret

13. Fret

F
C#
A
F

F
C#
A
F

A
F
C#
A
F

Fsus4

3. Fret

8. Fret

F
C
B♭
F
C
F

B♭
F
C
F

C
B♭
F
C
F

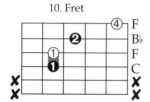

10. Fret

F
B♭
F
C

Fsus2

3. Fret

8. Fret

13. Fret

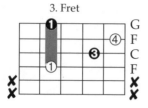

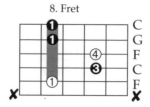

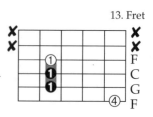

G
F
C
F

C
G
F
C
F

F
C
G
F

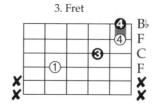

F♯

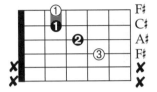
F♯
C♯
A♯
F♯

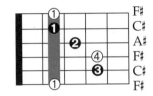
F♯
C♯
A♯
F♯
C♯
F♯

4. Fret

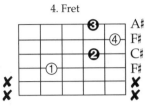
A♯
F♯
C♯
F♯

6. Fret

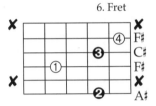
F♯
C♯
F♯
A♯

8. Fret

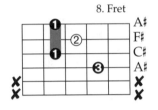
A♯
F♯
C♯
A♯

9. Fret

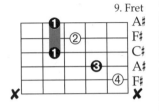
A♯
F♯
C♯
A♯
F♯

11. Fret

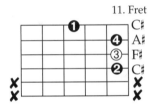
C♯
A♯
F♯
C♯

9. Fret

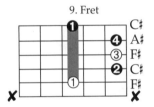
C♯
A♯
F♯
C♯
F♯

11. Fret

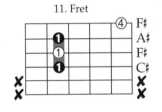
F♯
A♯
F♯
C♯

14. Fret

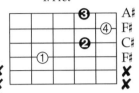
A♯
F♯
C♯
A♯
F♯

C

C♯/D♭

D

D♯/E♭

E

F

F♯/G♭

G

G♯/A♭

A

A♯/B♭

B

POWER CHORDS

SLASH CHORDS

TRANS-POSING

F#6

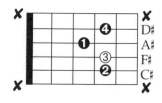

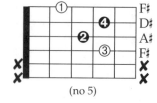

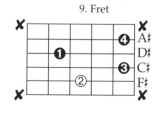

4. Fret

9. Fret

9. Fret

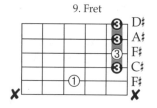

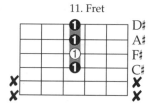

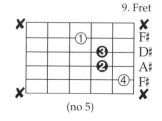

9. Fret

11. Fret

F#6/9

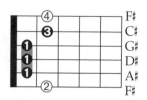

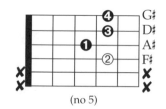

9. Fret

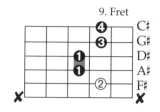

(no 5)

9. Fret

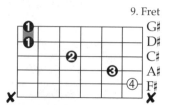

F♯maj7

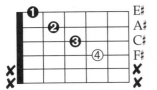
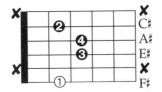
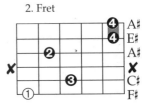

2. Fret

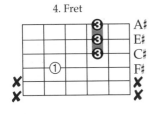
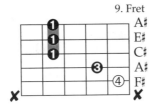
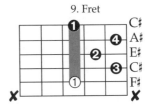

4. Fret   9. Fret   9. Fret

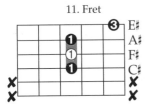

11. Fret

F♯maj13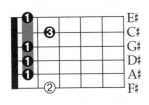

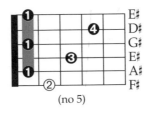
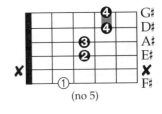

(no 5)   (no 5)

C
C♯/D♭
D
D♯/E♭
E
F
F♯/G♭
G
G♯/A♭
A
A♯/B♭
B
POWER CHORDS
SLASH CHORDS
TRANS- POSING

F♯maj9

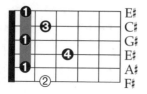

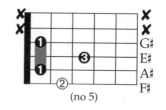
(no 5)

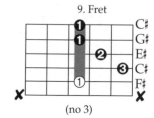
4. Fret
(no 5)

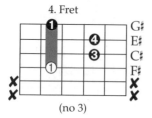
4. Fret
(no 3)

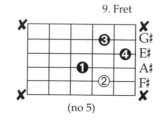
9. Fret
(no 5)

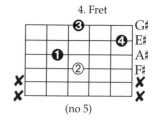
9. Fret
(no 3)

F♯maj9♯11

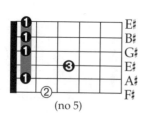
(no 5)

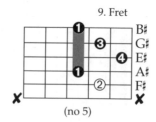
9. Fret
(no 5)

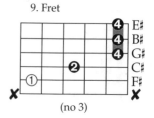
9. Fret
(no 3)

C
C♯/D♭
D
D♯/E♭
E
F
F♯/G♭
G
G♯/A♭
A
A♯/B♭
B
POWER CHORDS
SLASH CHORDS
TRANS-POSING

F♯maj7+

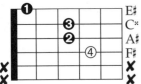

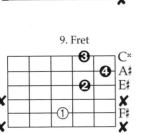

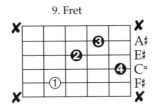

9. Fret

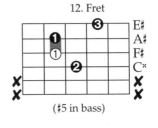

9. Fret

9. Fret

12. Fret

(♯5 in bass)

F♯maj7♭5

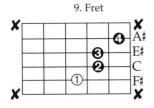

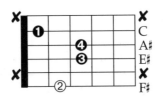

4. Fret

9. Fret

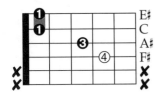

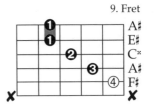

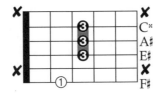

C

C♯/D♭

D

D♯/E♭

E

F

F♯/G♭

G

G♯/A♭

A

A♯/B♭

B

POWER CHORDS

SLASH CHORDS

TRANS-POSING

F#maj13(no9)

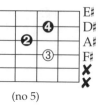

(no 5)

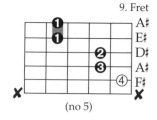

9. Fret

(no 5)

9. Fret

F#add9

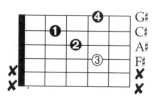

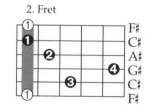

2. Fret

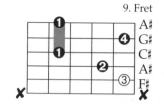

9. Fret

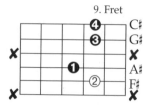

9. Fret

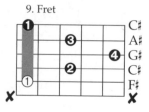

9. Fret

F♯m

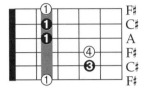

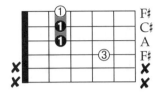

4. Fret

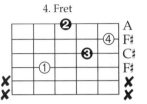

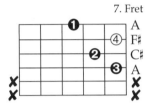

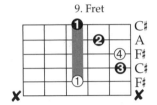

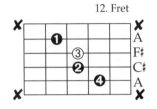

7. Fret

9. Fret

12. Fret

F♯m7

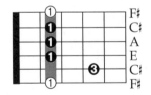

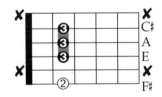

4. Fret

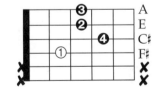

8. Fret

8. Fret

8. Fret

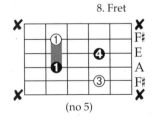
(no 5)

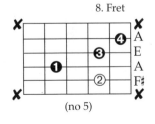
(no 5)

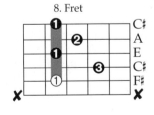

C

C♯/D♭

D

D♯/E♭

E

F

F♯/G♭

G

G♯/A♭

A

A♯/B♭

B

POWER CHORDS

SLASH CHORDS

TRANS-POSING

F♯m6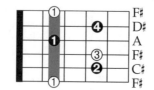

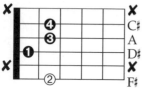

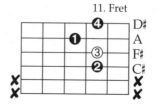

4. Fret

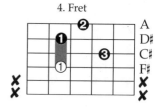

9. Fret

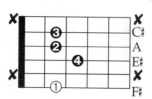

11. Fret

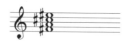

F♯m(maj7)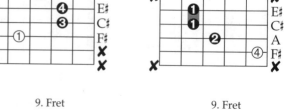

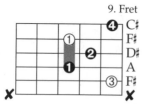

4. Fret

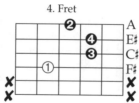

9. Fret

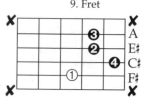

9. Fret

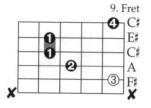

9. Fret

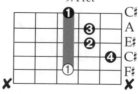

9. Fret

F#m add9

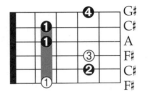

2. Fret

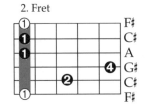

9. Fret

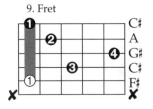

F#m9

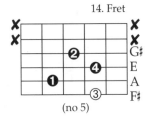

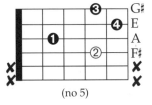

9. Fret

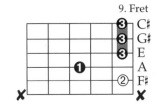

14. Fret

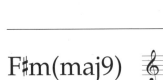

(no 5)

F#m(maj9)

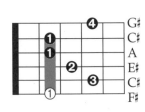

9. Fret

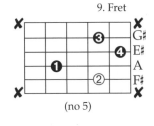

(no 5)

14. Fret

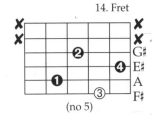

(no 5)

C
C♯/D♭
D
D♯/E♭
E
F
F♯/G♭
G
G♯/A♭
A
A♯/B♭
B
POWER CHORDS
SLASH CHORDS
TRANS-POSING

C

C♯/D♭

D

D♯/E♭

E

F

F♯/G♭

G

G♯/A♭

A

A♯/B♭

B

POWER
CHORDS

SLASH
CHORDS

TRANS-
POSING

F♯m 6/9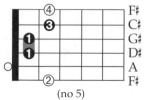

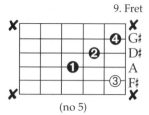 F♯ C♯ G♯ D♯ A F♯ (no 5)

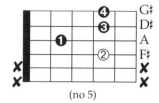 G♯ D♯ A F♯ (no 5)

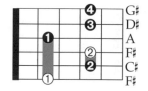 G♯ D♯ A F♯ C♯ F♯

9. Fret

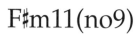 G♯ D♯ A F♯ (no 5)

F♯m11(no9)

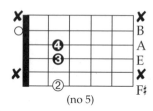 B A E F♯ (no 5)

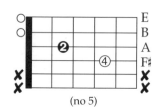 E B A F♯ (no 5)

9. Fret

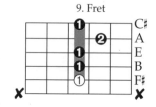 C♯ A E B F♯

F♯m11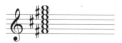

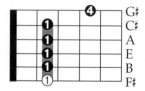 G♯ C♯ A E B F♯

F♯7

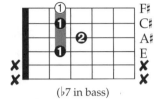

(♭7 in bass)

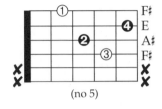

(no 5)

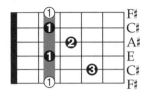

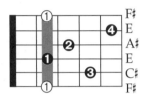

4. Fret

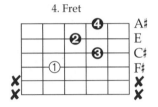

8. Fret

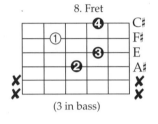

(3 in bass)

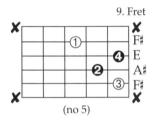

9. Fret

(no 5)

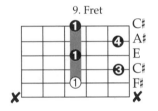

9. Fret

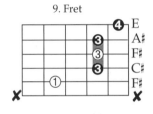

9. Fret

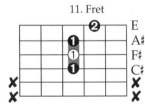

11. Fret

F#9

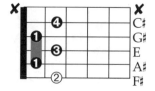

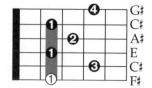

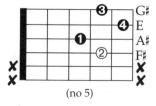

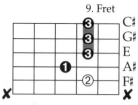

(no 5)

9. Fret

14. Fret

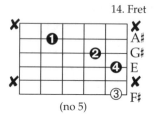

(no 5)

F#13

9. Fret

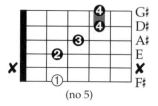

(no 5)

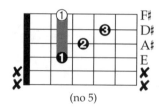

(no 5)

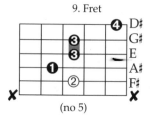

(no 5)

14. Fret

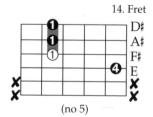

(no 5)

F#7♭9

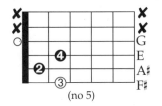 (no 5)

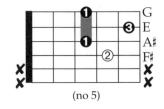 G E G E A# F# (no 5)

9. Fret

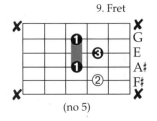 G E A# F# (no 5)

9. Fret

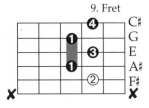 C# G E A# F#

F#7#9

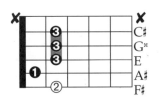 C# G× E A# F#

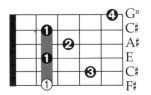 G× C# A# E C# F#

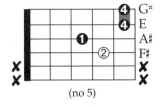 G× E A# F# (no 5)

9. Fret

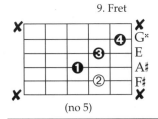 G× E A# F# (no 5)

F#13♭9

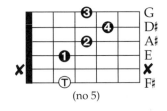 G D# A# E F# (no 5)

9. Fret

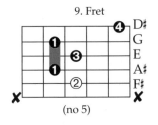 D# G E A# F# (no 5)

C
C#/D♭
D
D#/E♭
E
F
F#/G♭
G
G♭/A♭
A
A#/B♭
B
POWER CHORDS
SLASH CHORDS
TRANS-POSING

F#7+

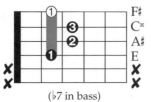

F#
C×
A#
E
×
×

(♭7 in bass)

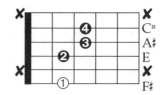

×   ×
C×
A#
E
×   ×
F#

4. Fret

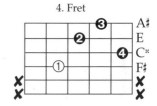

A#
E
C×
F#
×
×

9. Fret

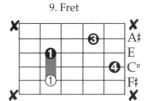

×   ×
A#
E
C×
F#
×

9. Fret

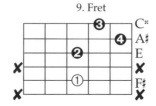

C×
A#
E
×
F#
×

F#7♭5

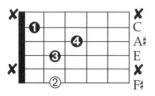

×
C
A#
E
×
F#

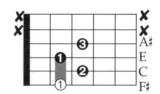

×   ×
×   ×
A#
E
C
F#

4. Fret

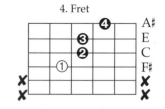

A#
E
C
F#
×
×

9. Fret

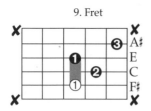

×   ×
A#
E
C
F#
×

10. Fret

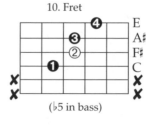

E
A#
F#
C
×
×

(♭5 in bass)

F♯7 ♭9 ♯5

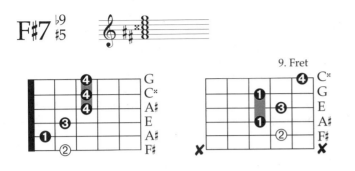

F7 ♯9 ♯5

F♯9♯11

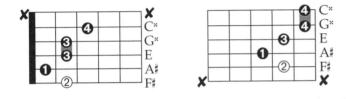

F♯9+

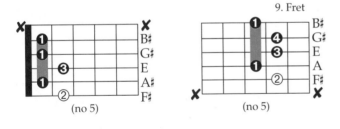

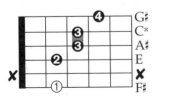

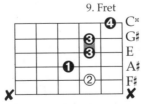

C
C♯/D♭
D
D♯/E♭
E
F
F♯/G♭
G
G♯/A♭
A
A♯/B♭
B
POWER CHORDS
SLASH CHORDS
TRANS-POSING

F♯7sus4

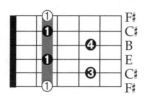

4. Fret

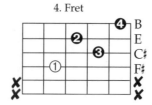

9. Fret

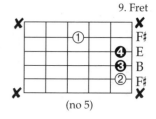

(no 5)

9. Fret

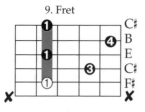

11. Fret

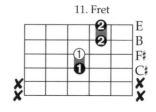

F♯9sus4

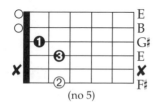

(no 5)

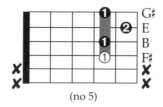

(no 5)

9. Fret

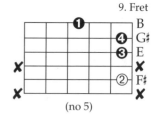

(no 5)

9. Fret

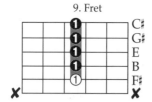

F♯13sus4

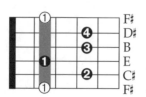

9. Fret

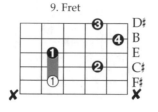

F#°

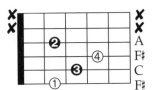 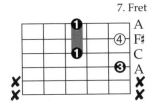 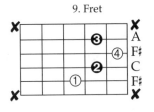

F#m7♭5

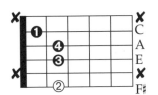 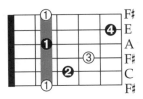 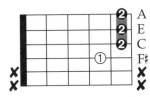

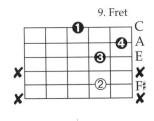 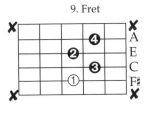

F#°7

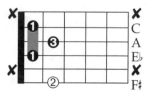

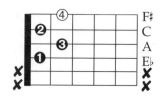

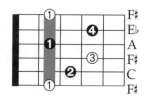

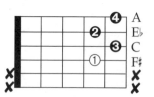

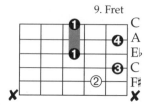

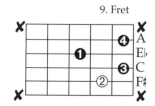

10. Fret

F♯+

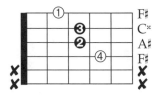

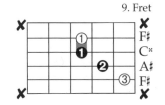

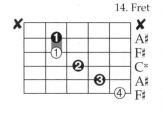

F♯sus4

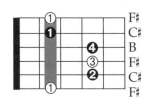

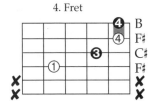

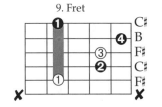

F♯sus2

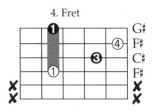

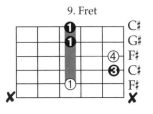

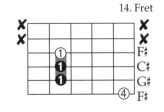

C

C♯/D♭

D

D♯/E♭

E

F

F♯/G♭

G

G♯/A♭

A

A♯/B♭

B

POWER CHORDS

SLASH CHORDS

TRANS-POSING

G

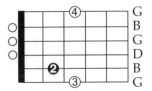

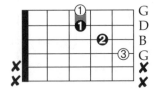

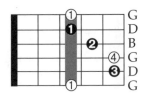

5. Fret

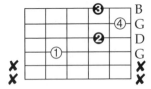

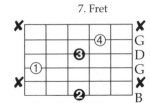

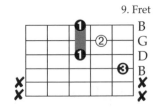

7. Fret   9. Fret

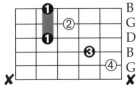

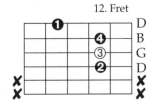

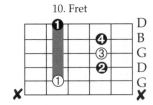

10. Fret   12. Fret   10. Fret

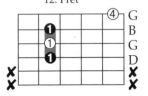

12. Fret

G6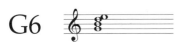

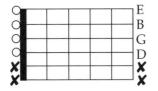
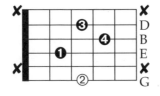
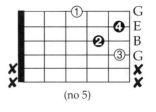

(no 5)

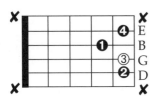

5. Fret
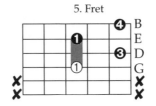

10. Fret
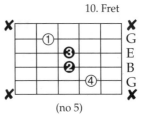

(no 5)

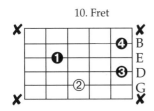

10. Fret
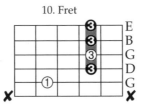

10. Fret

G $\frac{6}{9}$

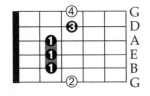

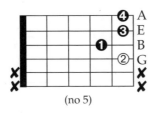
(no 5)

10. Fret
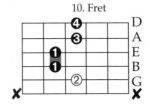

10. Fret
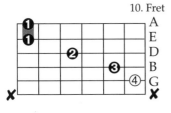

C

C#/Db

D

D#/Eb

E

F

F#/Gb

G

G#/Ab

A

A#/Bb

B

POWER CHORDS

SLASH CHORDS

TRANS- POSING

Gmaj7

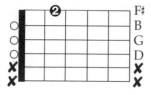
F#
B
G
D
X
X

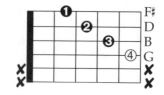
F#
D
B
G
X

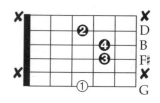
D
B
F#
G

3. Fret

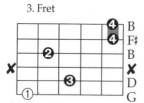
B
F#
B
D
G

5. Fret

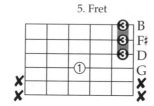
B
F#
D
G

10. Fret

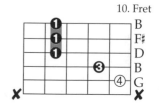
B
F#
D
B
G

10. Fret

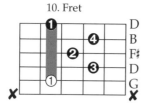
D
B
F#
D
G

Gmaj13

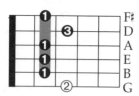
F#
D
A
E
B
G

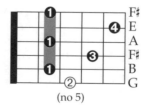
F#
E
A
F#
B
G

(no 5)

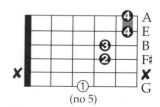
A
E
B
F#
G

(no 5)

Gmaj9

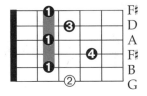

F#
D
A
F#
B
G

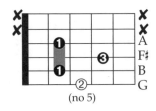

(no 5)

5. Fret

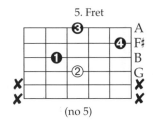

A
F#
B
G

(no 5)

5. Fret

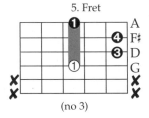

A
F#
D
G

(no 3)

10. Fret

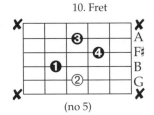

A
F#
B
G

(no 5)

10. Fret

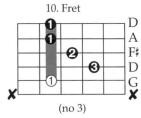

D
A
F#
D
G

(no 3)

Gmaj9♯11

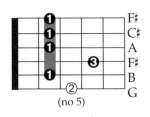

F#
C#
A
F#
B
G

(no 5)

10. Fret

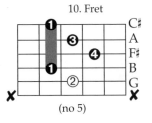

C#
A
F#
B
G

(no 5)

10. Fret

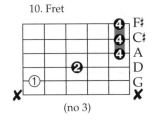

F#
C#
A
D
G

(no 3)

C

C♯/D♭

D

D♯/E♭

E

F

F♯/G♭

G

G♯/A♭

A

A♯/B♭

B

POWER CHORDS

SLASH CHORDS

TRANS-POSING

Gmaj7+

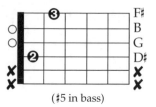
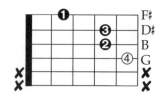
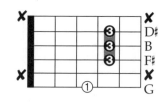

(♯5 in bass)

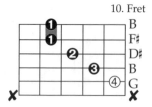
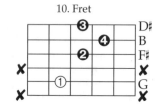
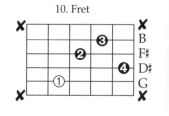

Gmaj7♭5

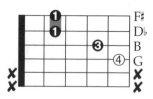
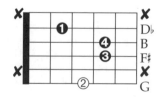
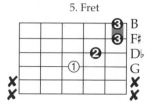

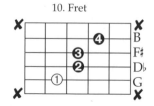

C
C♯/D♭
D
D♯/E♭
E
F
F♯/G♭
G
G♯/A♭
A
A♯/B♭
B
POWER CHORDS
SLASH CHORDS
TRANS-POSING

Gmaj13(no9)

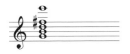

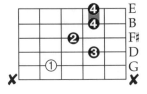

(no 5)

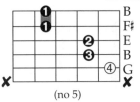

10. Fret

(no 5)

10. Fret

Gadd9

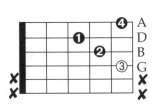

3. Fret

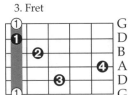

10. Fret

10. Fret

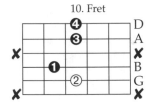

10. Fret

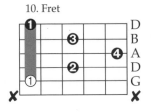

C
C♯/D♭
D
D♯/E♭
E
F
F♯/G♭
G
G♯/A♭
A
A♯/B♭
B
POWER CHORDS
SLASH CHORDS
TRANS- POSING

Gm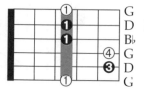

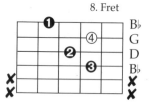 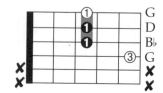 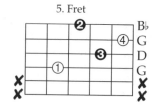

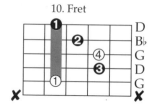 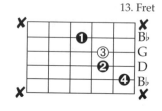

Gm7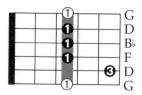

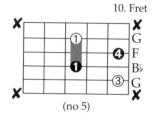 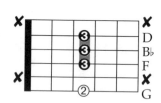 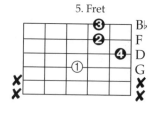

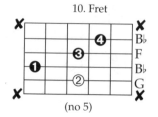 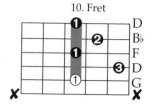

Gm6

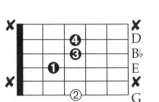

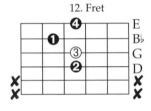

5. Fret

10. Fret

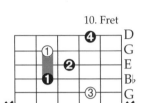

12. Fret

Gm(maj7)

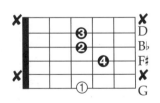

5. Fret

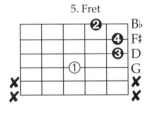

10. Fret

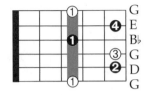

10. Fret

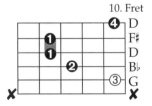

10. Fret

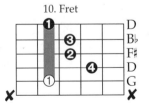

10. Fret

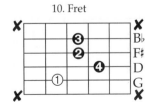

C
C#/Db
D
D#/Eb
E
F
F#/Gb
G
G#/Ab
A
A#/Bb
B
POWER CHORDS
SLASH CHORDS
TRANS-POSING

Gm add9

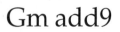

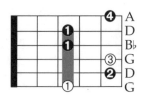

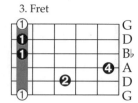

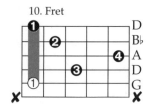

3. Fret

10. Fret

Gm9

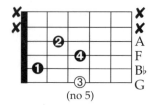

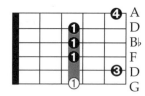

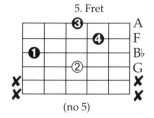

5. Fret

(no 5)

(no 5)

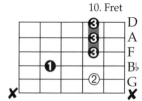

10. Fret

(no 5)

Gm(maj9)

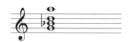

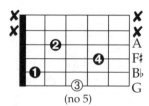

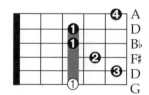

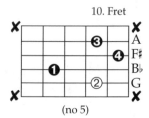

10. Fret

(no 5)

(no 5)

Gm $^6_9$

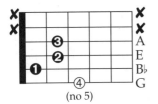
(no 5)

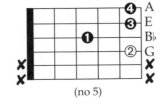
(no 5)

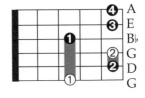

10. Fret

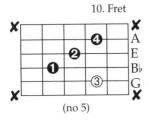
(no 5)

Gm11(no9)

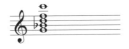

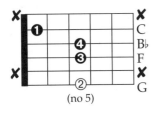
(no 5)

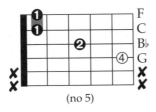
(no 5)

10. Fret

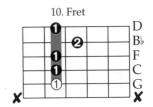

Gm11

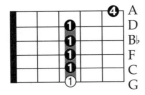

C

C#/Db

D

D#/Eb

E

F

F#/Gb

G

G#/Ab

A

A#/Bb

B

POWER CHORDS

SLASH CHORDS

TRANS- POSING

G7

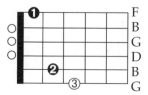
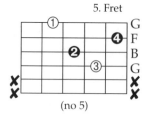

F
B
G
D
B
G

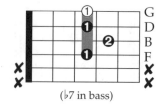

G
D
B
F

(♭7 in bass)

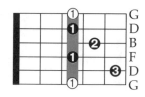
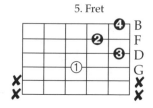

G
D
B
F
D
G

5. Fret

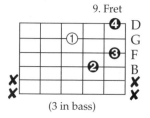

G
F
B
G

(no 5)

3. Fret

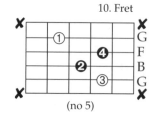

G
F
B
F
D
G

5. Fret

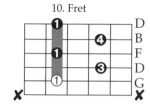

B
F
D
G

9. Fret

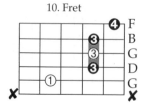

D
G
F
B

(3 in bass)

10. Fret

G
F
B
G

(no 5)

10. Fret

D
B
F
D
G

10. Fret

F
B
G
D
G

G9

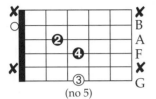
(no 5)

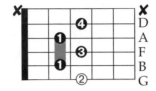

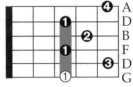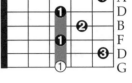

5. Fret

10. Fret

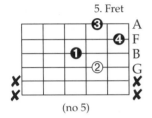
(no 5)

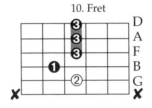

G13

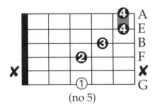
(no 5)

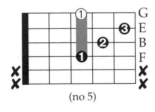
(no 5)

10. Fret

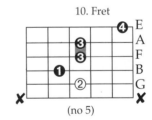
(no 5)

15. Fret

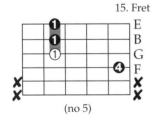
(no 5)

C

C♯/D♭

D

D♯/E♭

E

F

F♯/G♭

G

G♯/A♭

A

A♯/B♭

B

POWER CHORDS

SLASH CHORDS

TRANS- POSING

G7♭9

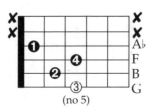
(no 5)

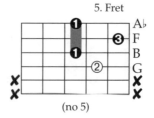
5. Fret
(no 5)

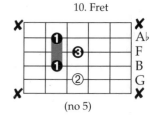
10. Fret
(no 5)

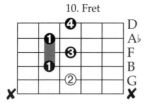
10. Fret

G7♯9

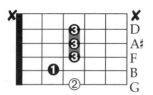

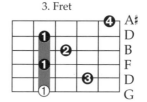
3. Fret

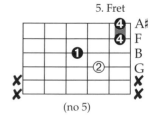
5. Fret
(no 5)

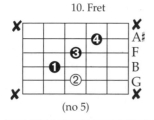
10. Fret
(no 5)

G13♭9

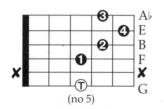
(no 5)

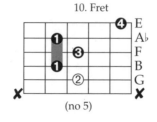
10. Fret
(no 5)

G7+

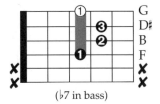

G
D#
B
F

(♭7 in bass)

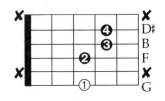

D#
B
F
G

5. Fret

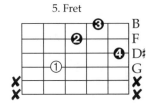

B
F
D#
G

10. Fret

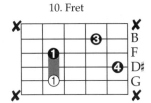

B
F
D#
G

10. Fret

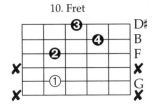

D#
B
F
G

G7♭5

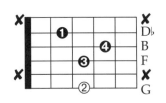

D♭
B
F
G

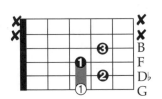

B
F
D♭
G

5. Fret

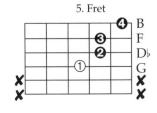

B
F
D♭
G

10. Fret

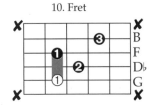

B
F
D♭
G

11. Fret

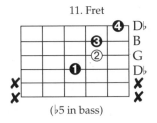

D♭
B
G
D♭

(♭5 in bass)

C
C#/D♭
D
D#/E♭
E
F
F#/G♭
G
G#/A♭
A
A#/B♭
B
POWER CHORDS
SLASH CHORDS
TRANS-POSING

G7 ♭9 ♯5

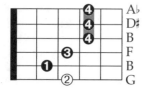

	A♭
	D♯
	B
	F
	B
	G

10. Fret

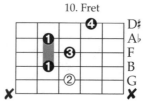

	D♯
	A♭
	F
	B
	G

G7 ♯9 ♯5

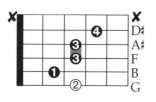

	D♯
	A♯
	F
	B
	G

10. Fret

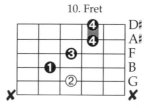

	D♯
	A♯
	F
	B
	G

G9♯11

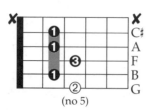

	C♯
	A
	F
	B
	G

(no 5)

10. Fret

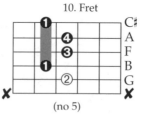

	C♯
	A
	F
	B
	G

(no 5)

G9+

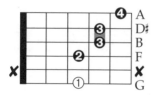

	A
	D♯
	B
	F
	G

10. Fret

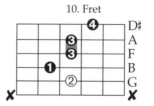

	D♯
	A
	F
	B
	G

G7sus4

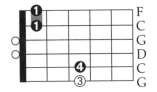
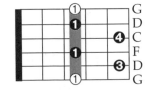
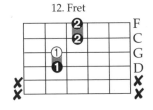

5. Fret

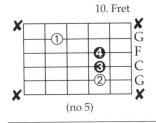
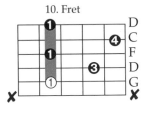
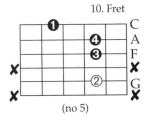

10. Fret | 10. Fret | 12. Fret

(no 5)

G9sus4

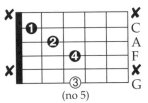
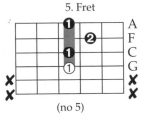

5. Fret | 10. Fret

(no 5) | (no 5) | (no 5)

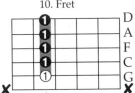

10. Fret

G13sus4

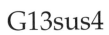

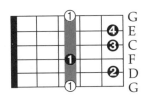
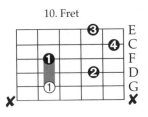

10. Fret

C
C#/Db
D
D#/Eb
E
F
F#/Gb
G
G#/Ab
A
A#/Bb
B
POWER CHORDS
SLASH CHORDS
TRANS-POSING

G°

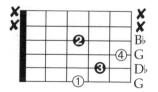
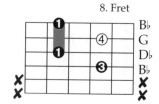
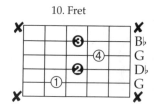

Gm7♭5

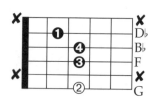
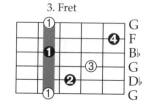
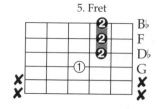

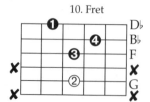
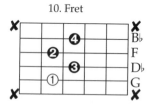

G°7

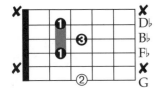

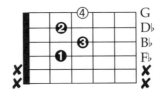

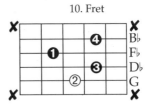

5. Fret

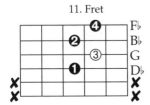

10. Fret

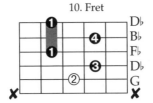

10. Fret

11. Fret

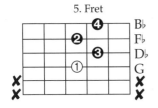

C

C#/Db

D

D#/Eb

E

F

F#/Gb

G

G#/Ab

A

A#/Bb

B

POWER
CHORDS

SLASH
CHORDS

TRANS-
POSING

C
C#/Db
D
D#/Eb
E
F
F#/Gb
G
G#/Ab
A
A#/Bb
B
POWER CHORDS
SLASH CHORDS
TRANS-POSING

G+

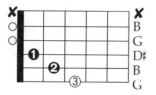

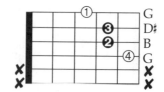

10. Fret

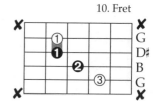

Gsus4

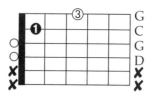

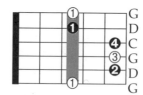

5. Fret

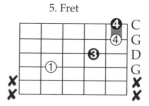

10. Fret

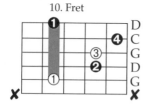

Gsus2

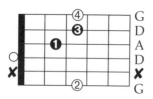

5. Fret

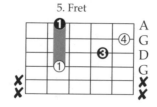

10. Fret

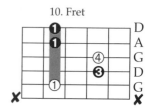

15. Fret

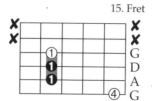

A♭

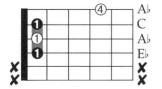

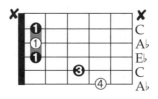

6. Fret

4. Fret

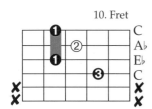

6. Fret

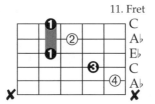

8. Fret

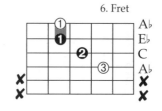

10. Fret

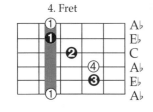

11. Fret

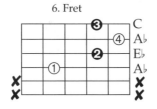

13. Fret

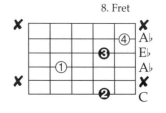

11. Fret

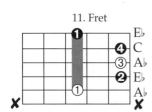

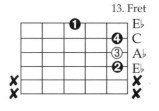

C

C♯/D♭

D

D♯/E♭

E

F

F♯/G♭

G

G♯/A♭

A

A♯/B♭

B

POWER CHORDS

SLASH CHORDS

TRANS- POSING

Ab6

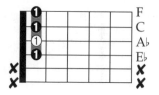

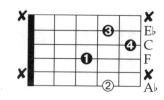

6. Fret

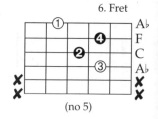
(no 5)

6. Fret

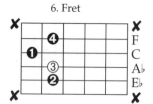

6. Fret

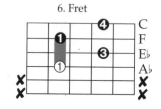

11. Fret

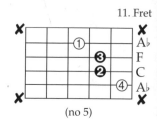
(no 5)

11. Fret

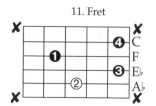

11. Fret

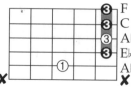

Ab⁶⁄₉

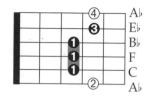

6. Fret

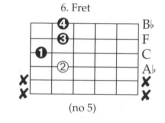
(no 5)

11. Fret

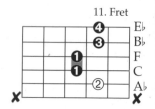

11. Fret

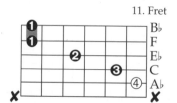

A♭maj7

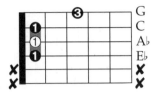
G
C
A♭
E♭

6. Fret
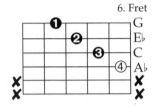
G
E♭
C
A♭

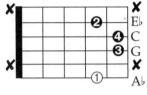
E♭
C
G
A♭

4. Fret
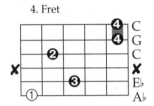
C
G
C
E♭
A♭

6. Fret
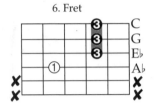
C
G
E♭
A♭

11. Fret
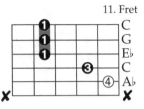
C
G
E♭
C
A♭

11. Fret
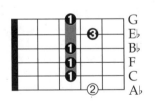
E♭
C
G
E♭
A♭

A♭maj13

G
E♭
B♭
F
C
A♭

4. Fret
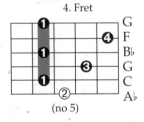
G
F
B♭
G
C
A♭
(no 5)

4. Fret
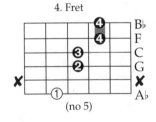
B♭
F
C
G
A♭
(no 5)

C

C♯/D♭

D

D♯/E♭

E

F

F♯/G♭

G

G♯/A♭

A

A♯/B♭

B

POWER CHORDS

SLASH CHORDS

TRANS-POSING

A♭maj9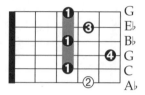

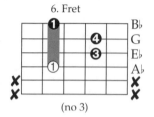

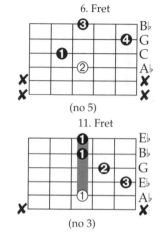

(no5)   (no 5)

(no 3)   (no 5)   (no 3)

A♭maj9♯11

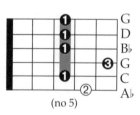

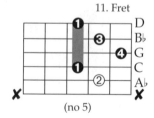

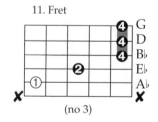

(no 5)   (no 5)   (no 3)

A♭maj7+

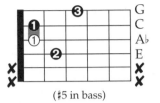

(♯5 in bass)

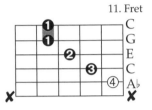

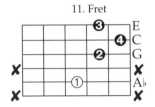

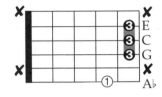

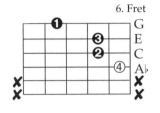

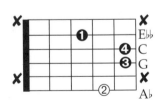

A♭maj7♭5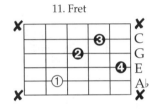

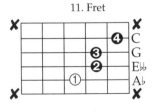

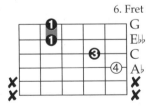

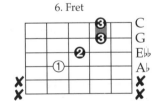

C · C♯/D♭ · D · D♯/E♭ · E · F · F♯/G♭ · G · G♯/A♭ · A · A♯/B♭ · B · POWER CHORDS · SLASH CHORDS · TRANS-POSING

A♭maj13(no9)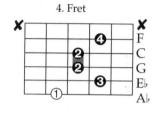

6. Fret
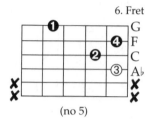

G
F
C
A♭

(no 5)

4. Fret
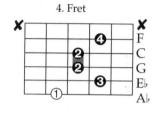

F
C
G
E♭
A♭

11. Fret
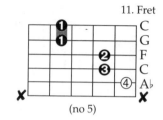

C
G
F
C
A♭

(no 5)

11. Fret
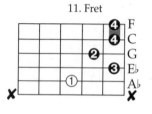

F
C
G
E♭
A♭

A♭add9

6. Fret
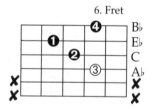

B♭
E♭
C
A♭

4. Fret
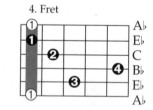

A♭
E♭
C
B♭
E♭
A♭

11. Fret
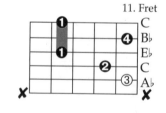

C
B♭
E♭
C
A♭

11. Fret
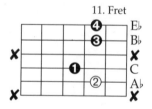

E♭
B♭
C
A♭

11. Fret
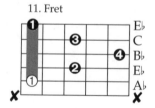

E♭
C
B♭
E♭
A♭

A♭m

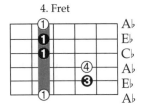

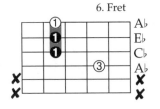

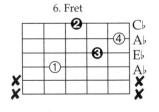

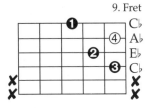

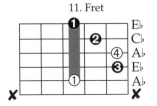

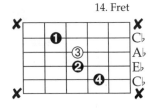

A♭m7

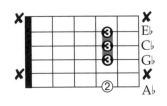

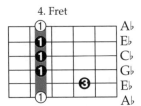

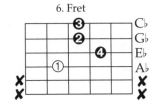

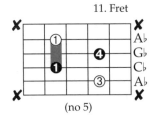
(no 5)

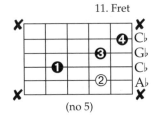
(no 5)

A♭m6

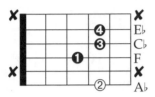

4. Fret

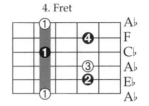

6. Fret

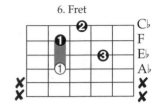

11. Fret

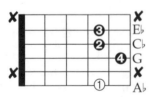

13. Fret

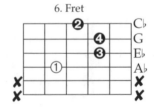

A♭m(maj7)

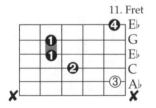

6. Fret

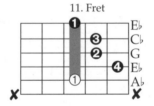

11. Fret

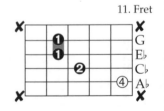

11. Fret

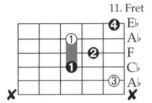

11. Fret

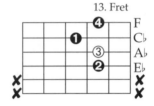

11. Fret

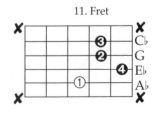

A♭m add9

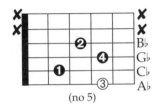

A♭m9

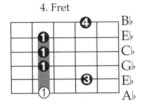

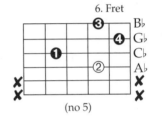

(no 5)

(no 5)

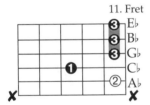

A♭m(maj9)

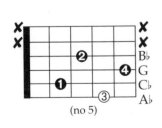

(no 5)

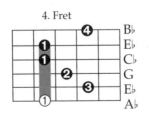

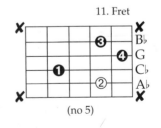

(no 5)

C

C♯/D♭

D

D♯/E♭

E

F

F♯/G♭

G

G♯/A♭

A

A♯/B♭

B

POWER CHORDS

SLASH CHORDS

TRANS-POSING

A♭m⁶₉

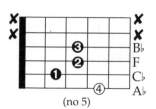

(no 5)

6. Fret

4 · B♭
3 · F
1 · C♭
2 · A♭

(no 5)

4. Fret

4 · B♭
3 · F
1 · C♭
2 · A♭
2 · E♭
1 · A♭

11. Fret

4 · B♭
2 · F
1 · C♭
3 · A♭

(no 5)

A♭m11(no9)

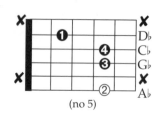

(no 5)

6. Fret

1 · G♭
1 · D♭
2 · C♭
4 · A♭

(no 5)

11. Fret

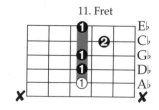

1 · E♭
2 · C♭
1 · G♭
1 · D♭
1 · A♭

A♭m11

4. Fret

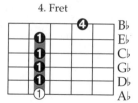

4 · B♭
1 · E♭
1 · C♭
1 · G♭
1 · D♭
1 · A♭

A♭7

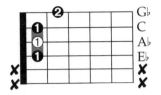

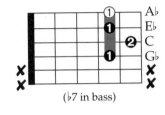

(♭7 in bass)

4. Fret

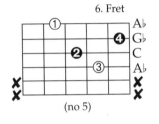

(no 5)

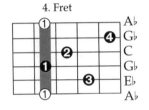

4. Fret

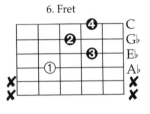

6. Fret

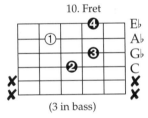

6. Fret

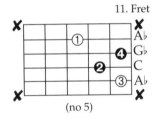

10. Fret

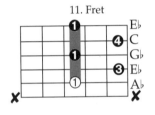

(3 in bass)

11. Fret

11. Fret

11. Fret

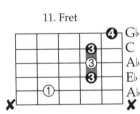

(no 5)

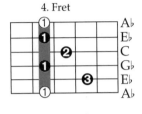

11. Fret

C

C♯/D♭

D

D♯/E♭

E

F

F♯/G♭

G

G♯/A♭

A

A♯/B♭

B

POWER CHORDS

SLASH CHORDS

TRANS- POSING

A♭9

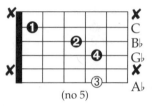

(no 5)

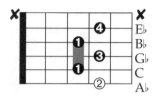

4. Fret
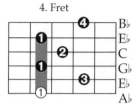

6. Fret
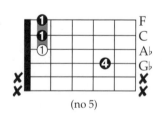

(no 5)

11. Fret
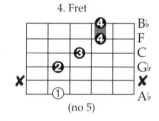

A♭13

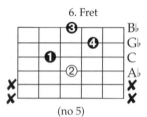

(no 5)

4. Fret
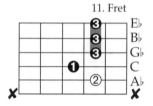

(no 5)

4. Fret
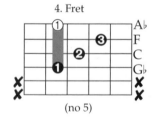

(no 5)

11. Fret
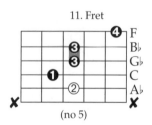

(no 5)

Ab7b9

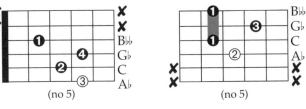

(no 5)   6. Fret (no 5)   11. Fret (no 5)

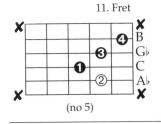

11. Fret

Ab7#9

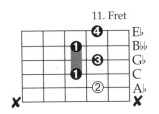

4. Fret   6. Fret (no 5)

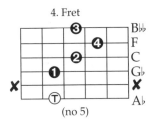

11. Fret (no 5)

Ab13b9

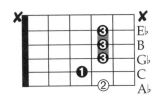

4. Fret (no 5)   11. Fret (no 5)

C
C#/Db
D
D#/Eb
E
F
F#/Gb
G
G#/Ab
A
A#/Bb
B
POWER CHORDS
SLASH CHORDS
TRANS-POSING

A♭7+

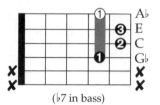

(♭7 in bass)

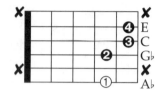

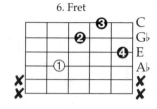

6. Fret

11. Fret

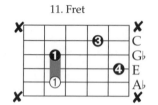

11. Fret

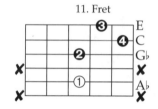

A♭7♭5

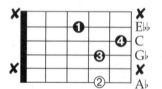

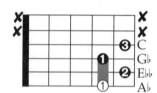

6. Fret

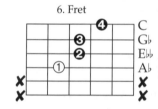

11. Fret

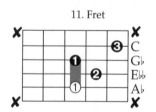

10. Fret

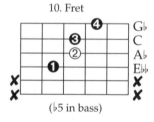

(♭5 in bass)

Ab7 b9/#5

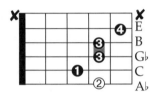

11. Fret

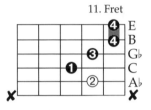

Ab7 #9/#5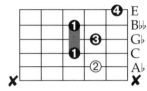

11. Fret

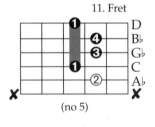

Ab9#11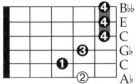

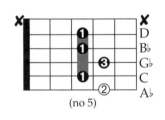

(no 5)

11. Fret

(no 5)

Ab9+

4. Fret

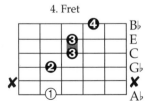

11. Fret

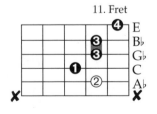

C
C#/Db
D
D#/Eb
E
F
F#/Gb
G
G#/Ab
A
A#/Bb
B
POWER CHORDS
SLASH CHORDS
TRANS-POSING

A♭7sus4

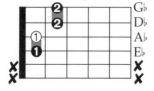

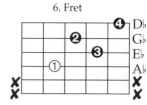

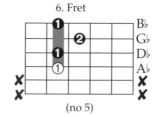

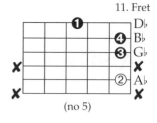

(no 5)

A♭9sus4

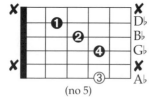

(no 5)

(no 5)

(no 5)

A♭13sus4

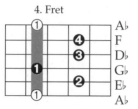

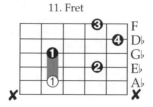

Ab°

4. Fret

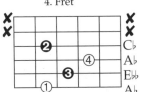

9. Fret

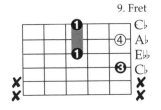

11. Fret

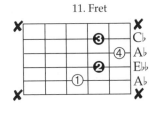

Abm7b5

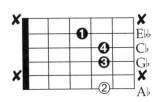

4. Fret

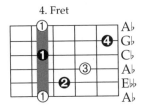

6. Fret

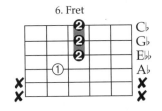

11. Fret

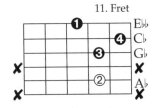

11. Fret

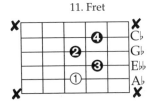

C

C#/Db

D

D#/Eb

E

F

F#/Gb

G

G#/Ab

A

A#/Bb

B

POWER CHORDS

SLASH CHORDS

TRANS- POSING

A♭°7

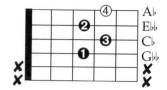

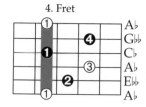

4. Fret

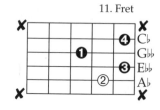

6. Fret

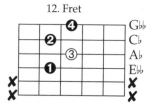

11. Fret

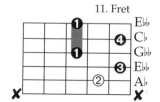

11. Fret

12. Fret

A♭+

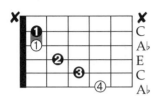

6. Fret

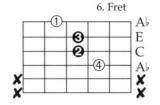

11. Fret

A♭sus4

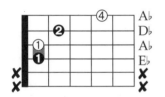

4. Fret

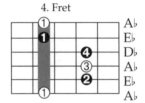

6. Fret

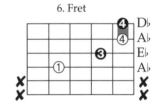

11. Fret

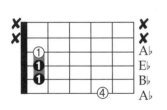

A♭sus2

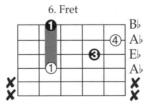

6. Fret

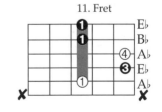

11. Fret

C

C♯/D♭

D

D♯/E♭

E

F

F♯/G♭

G

G♯/A♭

A

A♯/B♭

B

POWER CHORDS

SLASH CHORDS

TRANS-POSING

A

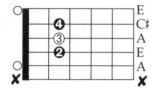

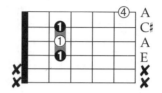

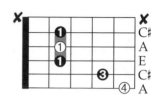

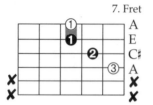

7. Fret

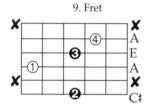

5. Fret

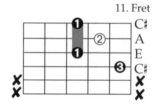

7. Fret

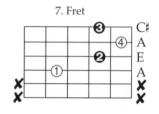

9. Fret

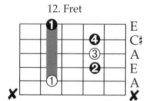

11. Fret

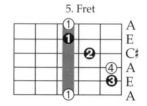

12. Fret

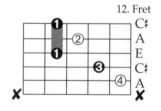

12. Fret

C
C♯/D♭
D
D♯/E♭
E
F
F♯/G♭
G
G♯/A♭
A
A♯/B♭
B
POWER CHORDS
SLASH CHORDS
TRANS- POSING

A6

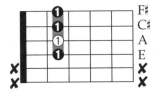

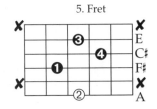
5. Fret

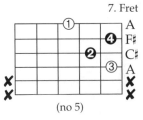
7. Fret

(no 5)

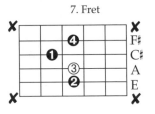
7. Fret

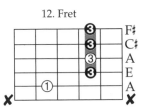
7. Fret

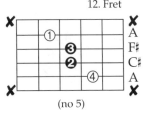
12. Fret

(no 5)

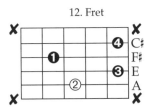
12. Fret

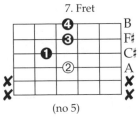
12. Fret

A $\frac{6}{9}$

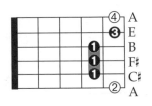

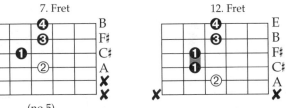
7. Fret

(no 5)

12. Fret

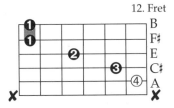
12. Fret

C

C♯/D♭

D

D♯/E♭

E

F

F♯/G♭

G

G♯/A♭

A

A♯/B♭

B

POWER
CHORDS

SLASH
CHORDS

TRANS-
POSING

Amaj7

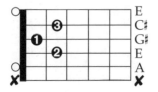 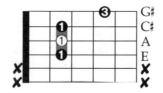 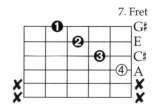

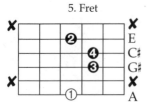 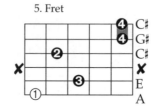 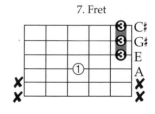

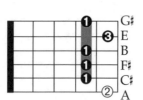

Amaj13

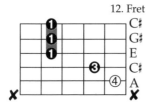 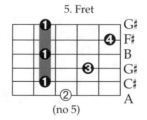 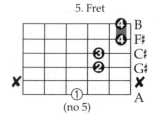

Amaj9

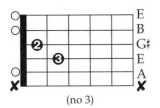
(no 3)

5. Fret
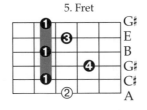

5. Fret
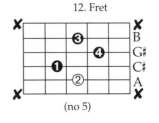

7. Fret
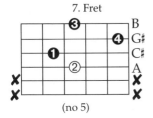
(no 5)

7. Fret
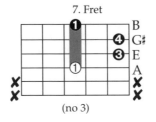
(no 3)

12. Fret
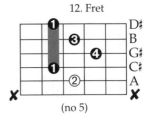
(no 5)

Amaj9♯11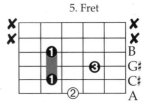

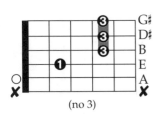
(no 3)

5. Fret

(no 5)

12. Fret
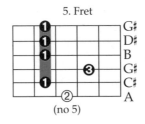
(no 5)

C

C♯/D♭

D

D♯/E♭

E

F

F♯/G♭

G

G♯/A♭

A

A♯/B♭

B

POWER CHORDS

SLASH CHORDS

TRANS-POSING

Amaj7+

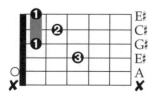
E#
C#
G#
E#
A

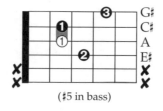
G#
C#
A
E#

(#5 in bass)

5. Fret
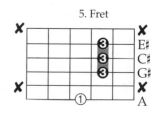
E#
C#
G#
A

7. Fret
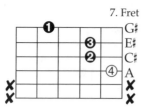
G#
E#
C#
A

12. Fret
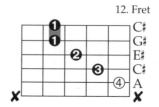
C#
G#
E#
C#
A

12. Fret
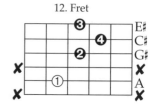
E#
C#
G#
A

Amaj7♭5

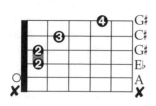
G#
C#
G#
E♭
A

5. Fret
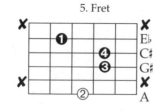
G#
E♭
C#
G#
A

7. Fret
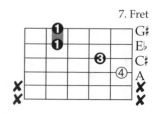
G#
E♭
C#
A

7. Fret
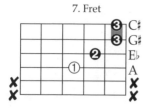
C#
G#
E♭
A

Amaj13(no9)

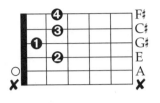

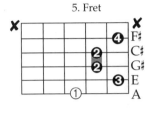

7. Fret

5. Fret

(no 5)

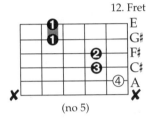

12. Fret

(no 5)

Aadd9

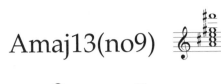

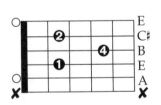

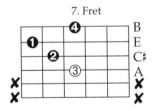

7. Fret

5. Fret

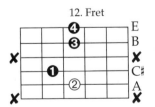

12. Fret

12. Fret

C

C♯/D♭

D

D♯/E♭

E

F

F♯/G♭

G

G♯/A♭

A

A♯/B♭

B

POWER CHORDS

SLASH CHORDS

TRANS- POSING

Am

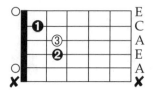

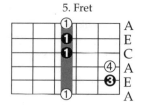

5. Fret

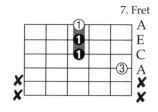

7. Fret

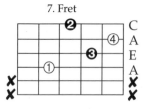

7. Fret

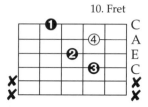

10. Fret

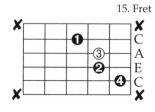

15. Fret

Am7

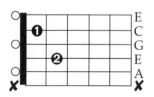

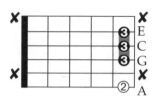

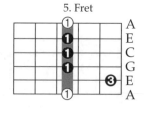

5. Fret

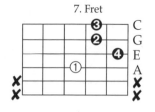

7. Fret

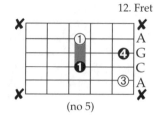

12. Fret

(no 5)

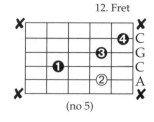

12. Fret

(no 5)

Am6

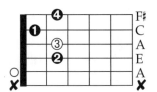
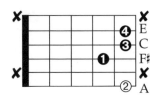
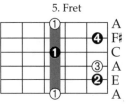

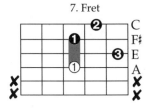
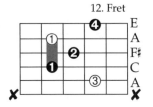

Am(maj7)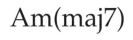

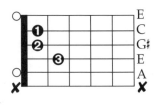
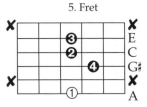
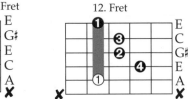

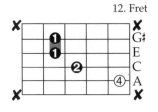
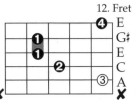

Am add9

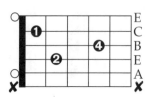

5. Fret
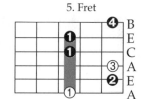

5. Fret
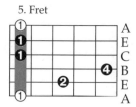

Am9

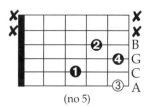
(no 5)

5. Fret
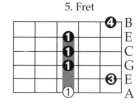

7. Fret
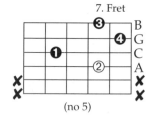
(no 5)

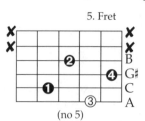

Am(maj9)

5. Fret

(no 5)

5. Fret
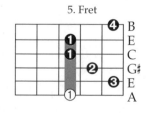

12. Fret
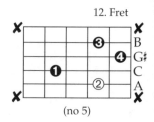
(no 5)

Am $^6_9$

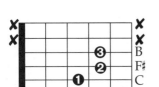

7. Fret

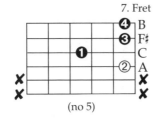
(no 5)

5. Fret

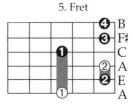

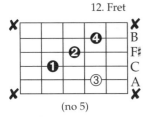
(no 5)

12. Fret

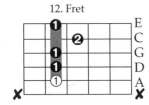
(no 5)

Am11(no9)

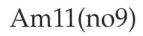

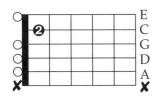

(no 5)

7. Fret

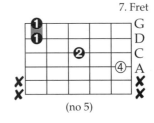
(no 5)

12. Fret

Am11

5. Fret

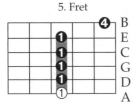

C

C♯/D♭

D

D♯/E♭

E

F

F♯/G♭

G

G♯/A♭

A

A♯/B♭

B

POWER CHORDS

SLASH CHORDS

TRANS-POSING

A7

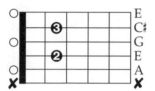
E
C#
G
E
A

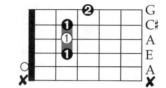
G
C#
A
E
A

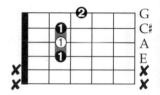
G
C#
A
E

5. Fret

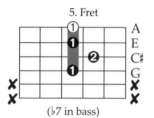
A
E
C#
G

(♭7 in bass)

5. Fret

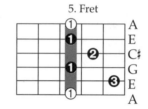
A
E
C#
G
E
A

7. Fret

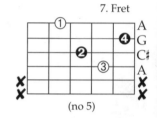
A
G
C#
A

(no 5)

5. Fret

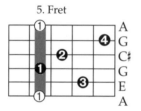
A
G
C#
G
E
A

7. Fret

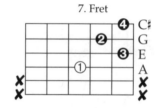
C#
G
E
A

11. Fret

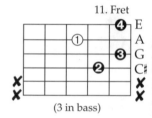
E
A
G
C#

(3 in bass)

12. Fret

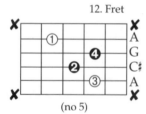
A
G
C#
A

(no 5)

A9

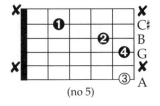

(no 5)

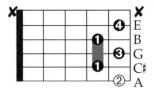

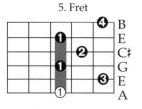

5. Fret

7. Fret

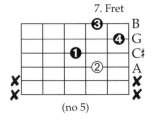

(no 5)

12. Fret

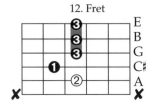

A13

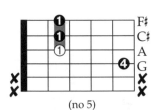

(no 5)

5. Fret

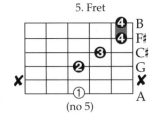

(no 5)

5. Fret

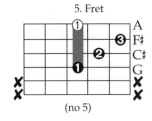

(no 5)

12. Fret

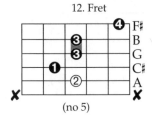

(no 5)

C
C#/Db
D
D#/Eb
E
F
F#/Gb
G
G#/Ab
A
A#/Bb
B
POWER CHORDS
SLASH CHORDS
TRANS-POSING

A7♭9

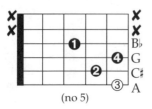
(no 5)

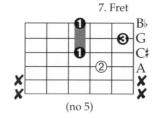
7. Fret
(no 5)

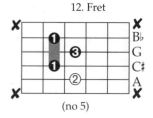
12. Fret
(no 5)

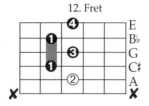
12. Fret

A7♯9

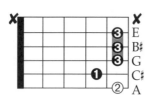
(no 5)

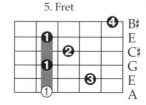
5. Fret

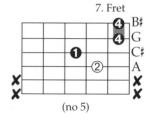
7. Fret
(no 5)

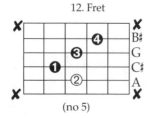
12. Fret
(no 5)

A13♭9

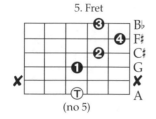
5. Fret
(no 5)

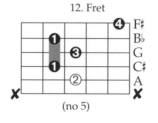
12. Fret
(no 5)

A7+

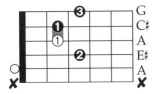

G
C#
A
E#
A

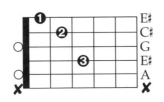

E#
C#
G
E#
A

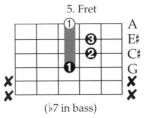

5. Fret

A
E#
C#
G

(♭7 in bass)

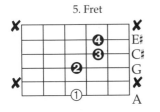

5. Fret

E#
C#
G
A

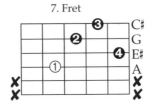

7. Fret

C#
G
E#
A

A7♭5

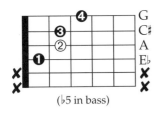

G
C#
A
E♭

(♭5 in bass)

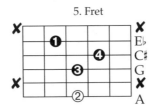

5. Fret

E♭
C#
G
A

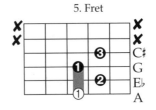

5. Fret

C#
G
E♭
A

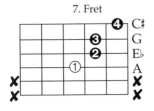

7. Fret

C#
G
E♭
A

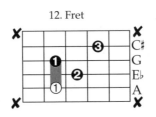

12. Fret

C#
G
E♭
A

C
C#/D♭
D
D#/E♭
E
F
F#/G♭
G
G#/A♭
A
A#/B♭
B
POWER CHORDS
SLASH CHORDS
TRANS-POSING

A7 ♭9 ♯5

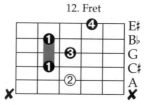
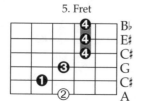

5. Fret — B♭ E♯ C♯ G C♯ A

12. Fret — E♯ B♭ G C♯ A

A7 ♯9 ♯5

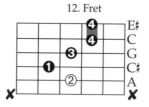
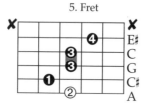

5. Fret — E♯ C G C♯ A

12. Fret — E♯ C G C♯ A

A9♯11

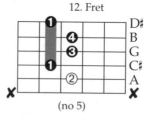
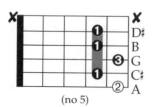

(no 5) — D♯ B G C♯ A

12. Fret (no 5) — D♯ B G C♯ A

A9+

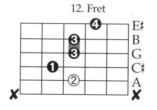
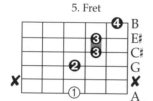

5. Fret — B E♯ C♯ G A

12. Fret — E♯ B G C♯ A

A7sus4

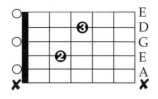

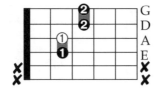

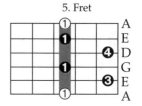

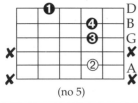

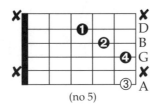

A9sus4

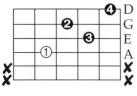

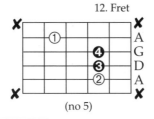

(no 5)

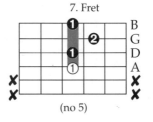

(no 5)

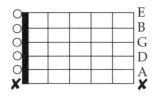

(no 5)

A13sus4

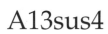

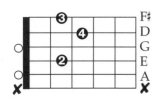

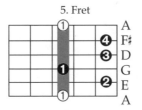

C

C#/Db

D

D#/Eb

E

F

F#/Gb

G

G#/Ab

A

A#/Bb

B

POWER CHORDS

SLASH CHORDS

TRANS-POSING

A°

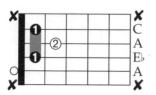

5. Fret

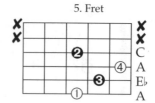

10. Fret

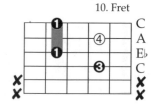

Am7♭5

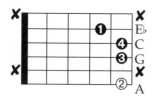

5. Fret

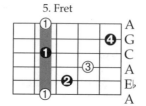

7. Fret

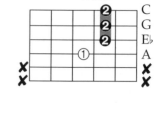

12. Fret

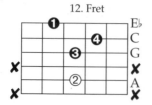

12. Fret

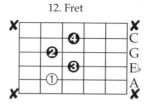

A°7

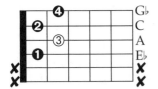

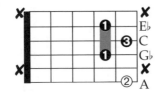

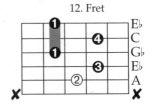

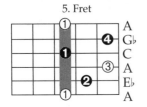

5. Fret

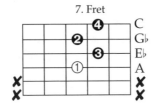

7. Fret

12. Fret

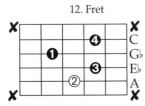

12. Fret

C
C♯/D♭
D
D♯/E♭
E
F
F♯/G♭
G
G♯/A♭
A
A♯/B♭
B
POWER CHORDS
SLASH CHORDS
TRANS-POSING

A+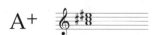

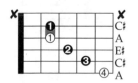
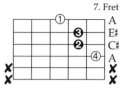
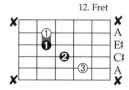

Asus4

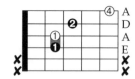
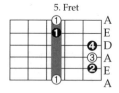

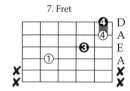

Asus2

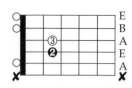
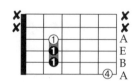
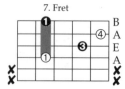

B♭

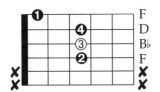

3. Fret

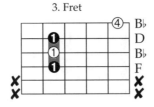

6. Fret

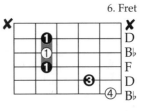

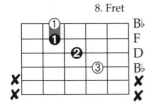

8. Fret

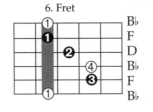

6. Fret

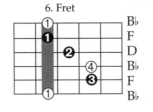

8. Fret

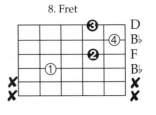

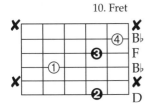

10. Fret

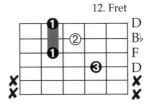

12. Fret

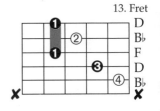

13. Fret

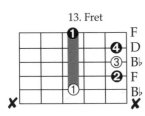

13. Fret

C

C♯/D♭

D

D♯/E♭

E

F

F♯/G♭

G

G♯/A♭

A

A♯/B♭

B

POWER CHORDS

SLASH CHORDS

TRANS- POSING

Bb6

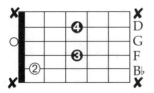

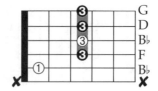

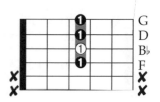

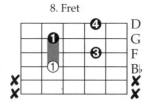
6. Fret

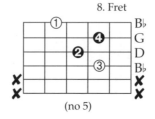
8. Fret

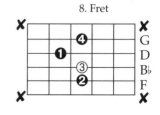
8. Fret

8. Fret

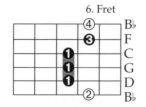
13. Fret

Bb 6/9

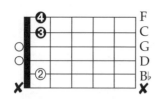

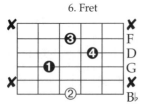
6. Fret

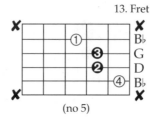
8. Fret

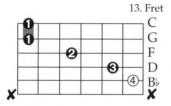
13. Fret

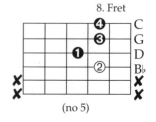

B♭maj7

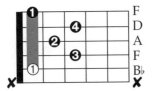
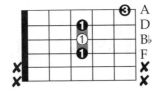
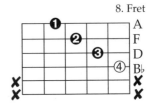

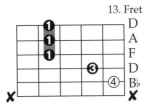
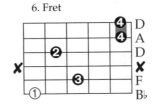
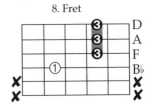

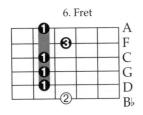

B♭maj13

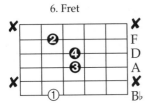
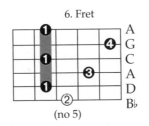
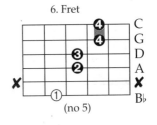

B♭maj9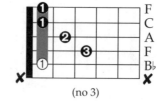

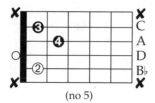

(no 5)

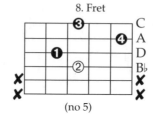

(no 3)

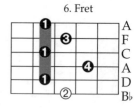

6. Fret

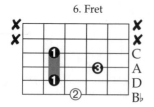

6. Fret

(no 5)

8. Fret

(no 5)

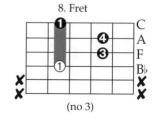

8. Fret

(no 3)

B♭maj9♯11

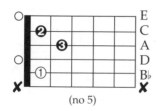

(no 5)

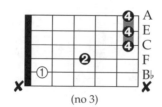

(no 3)

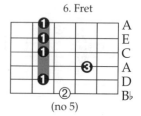

6. Fret

(no 5)

B♭maj7+

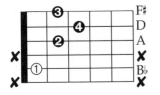

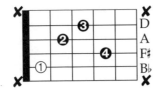

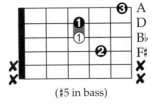

(♯5 in bass)

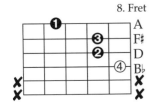

8. Fret

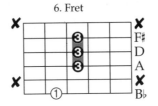

6. Fret

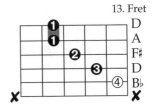

13. Fret

B♭maj7♭5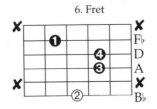

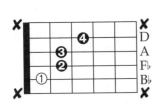

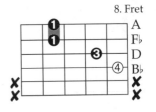

6. Fret

8. Fret

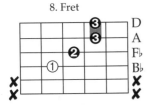

8. Fret

C

C♯/D♭

D

D♯/E♭

E

F

F♯/G♭

G

G♯/A♭

A

A♯/B♭

B

POWER CHORDS

SLASH CHORDS

TRANS-POSING

B♭maj13(no9)

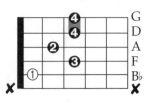
G
D
A
F
B♭

8. Fret
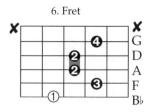
A
G
D
B♭
(no 5)

6. Fret
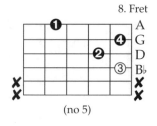
G
D
A
F
B♭

13. Fret
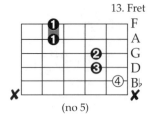
F
A
G
D
B♭
(no 5)

B♭add9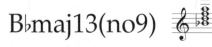

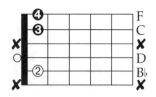
F
C
D
B♭

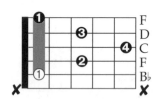
F
D
C
F
B♭

8. Fret
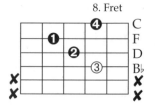
C
F
D
B♭

6. Fret
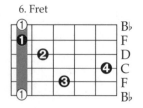
B♭
F
D
C
F
B♭

13. Fret
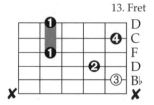
D
C
F
D
B♭

B♭m

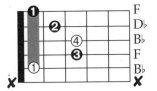

F
D♭
B♭
F
B♭

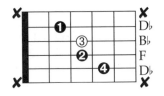

D♭
B♭
F
D♭

6. Fret

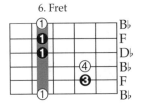

B♭
F
D♭
B♭
F
B♭

8. Fret

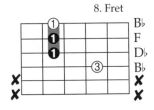

B♭
F
D♭
B♭

8. Fret

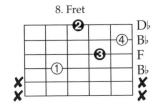

D♭
B♭
F
B♭

11. Fret

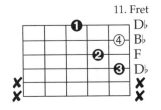

D♭
B♭
F
D♭

B♭m7

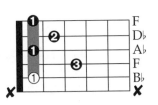

F
D♭
A♭
F
B♭

6. Fret

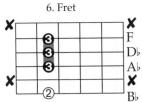

F
D♭
A♭
B♭

6. Fret

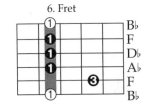

B♭
F
D♭
A♭
F
B♭

8. Fret

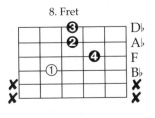

D♭
A♭
F
B♭

13. Fret

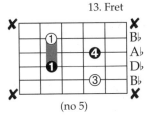

B♭
A♭
D♭
B♭

(no 5)

13. Fret

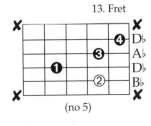

D♭
A♭
D♭
B♭

(no 5)

C

C♯/D♭

D

D♯/E♭

E

F

F♯/G♭

G

G♯/A♭

A

A♯/B♭

B

POWER CHORDS

SLASH CHORDS

TRANS- POSING

B♭m6

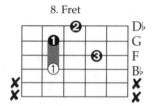

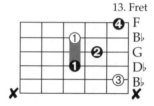

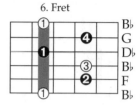

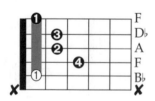

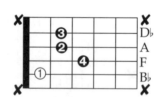

B♭m(maj7)

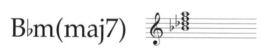

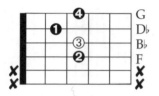

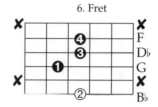

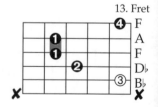

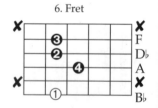

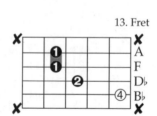

B♭m add9

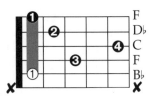
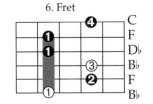
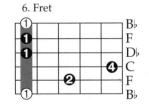

B♭m9

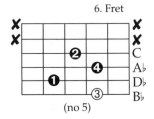
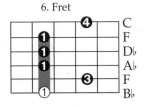
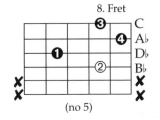
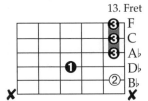

B♭m(maj9)

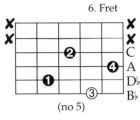
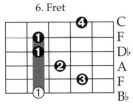
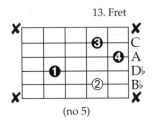

C   C♯/D♭   D   D♯/E♭   E   F   F♯/G♭   G   G♯/A♭   A   A♯/B♭   B   POWER CHORDS   SLASH CHORDS   TRANS-POSING

B♭m 6/9

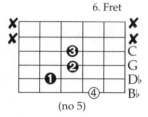

6. Fret
× ×
× — C
G
D♭
B♭
(no 5)

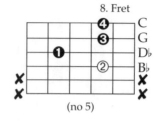

8. Fret
C
G
D♭
B♭
(no 5)

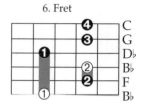

6. Fret
C
G
D♭
B♭
F
B♭

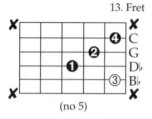

13. Fret
C
G
D♭
B♭
(no 5)

B♭m11(no9)

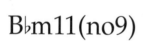

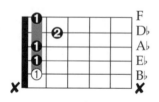

F
D♭
A♭
E♭
B♭

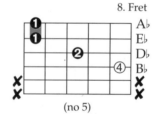

8. Fret
A♭
E♭
D♭
B♭
(no 5)

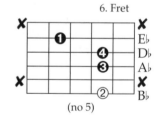

6. Fret
× — ×
E♭
D♭
A♭
× — ×
B♭
(no 5)

B♭m11

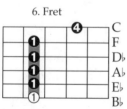

6. Fret
C
F
D♭
A♭
E♭
B♭

C
C♯/D♭
D
D♯/E♭
E
F
F♯/G♭
G
G♯/A♭
A
A♯/B♭
B
POWER CHORDS
SLASH CHORDS
TRANS-POSING

B♭7

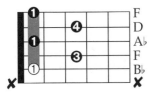

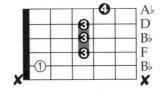

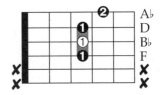

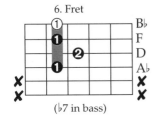

6. Fret

(♭7 in bass)

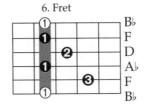

6. Fret

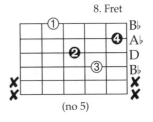

8. Fret

(no 5)

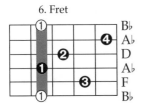

6. Fret

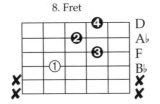

8. Fret

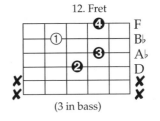

12. Fret

(3 in bass)

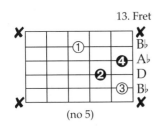

13. Fret

(no 5)

C
C#/D♭
D
D#/E♭
E
F
F#/G♭
G
G#/A♭
A
A#/B♭
B
POWER CHORDS
SLASH CHORDS
TRANS-POSING

B♭9

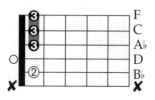

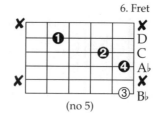
6. Fret
(no 5)

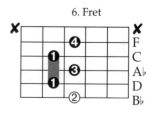
6. Fret

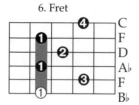
6. Fret

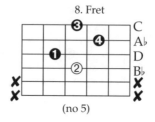
8. Fret
(no 5)

B♭13

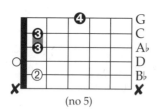
(no 5)

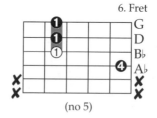
6. Fret
(no 5)

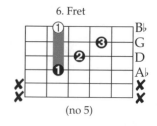
6. Fret
(no 5)

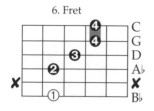
6. Fret

B♭7♭9

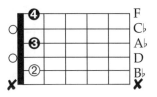

F
C♭
A♭
D
B♭

6. Fret

C♭
A♭
D
B♭

(no 5)

8. Fret

C♭
A♭
D♭
B♭

(no 5)

13. Fret

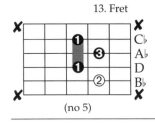

C♭
A♭
D
B♭

(no 5)

B♭7♯9

6. Fret

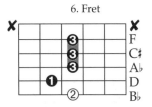

F
C♯
A♭
D
B♭

6. Fret

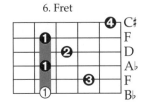

C♯
F
D
A♭
F
B♭

8. Fret

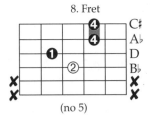

C♯
A♭
D
B♭

(no 5)

13. Fret

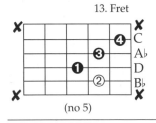

C
A♭
D
B♭

(no 5)

B♭13♭9

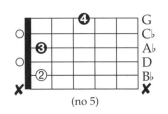

G
C♭
A♭
D
B♭

(no 5)

6. Fret

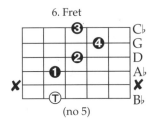

C♭
G
D
A♭
B♭

(no 5)

C
C♯/D♭
D
D♯/E♭
E
F
F♯/G♭
G
G♯/A♭
A
A♯/B♭
B
POWER CHORDS
SLASH CHORDS
TRANS-POSING

B♭7+

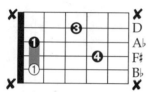

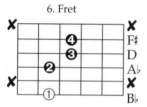

6. Fret

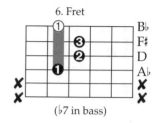

(♭7 in bass)

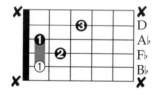

B♭7♭5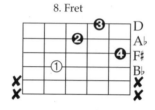

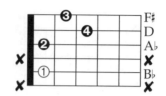

(♭5 in bass)

6. Fret

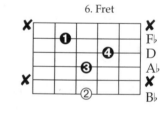

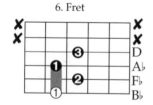

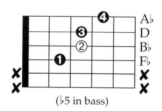

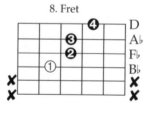

B♭7 ♭9/♯5

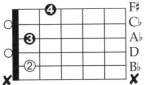

6. Fret

B♭7 ♯9/♯5

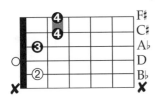

6. Fret

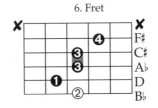

B♭9♯11

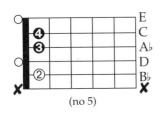

(no 5)

6. Fret

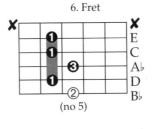

(no 5)

B♭9+

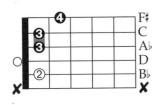

6. Fret

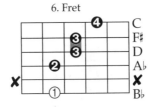

C
C♯/D♭
D
D♯/E♭
E
F
F♯/G♭
G
G♯/A♭
A
A♯/B♭
B
POWER CHORDS
SLASH CHORDS
TRANS-POSING

B♭7sus4

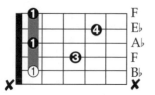

F
E♭
A♭
F
B♭

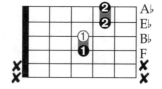

A♭
E♭
B♭
F

6. Fret

B♭
F
E♭
A♭
F
B♭

8. Fret

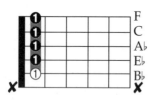

E♭
A♭
F
B♭

13. Fret

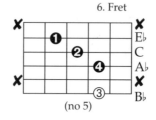

B♭
A♭
E♭
B♭

(no 5)

B♭9sus4

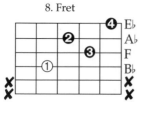

F
C
A♭
E♭
B♭

6. Fret

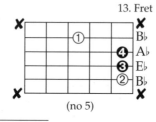

E♭
C
A♭
B♭

(no 5)

8. Fret

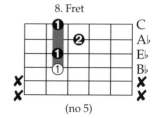

C
A♭
E♭
B♭

(no 5)

13. Fret

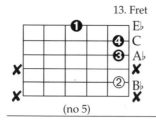

E♭
C
A♭
B♭

(no 5)

B♭13sus4

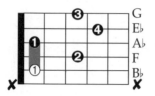

G
E♭
A♭
F
B♭

6. Fret

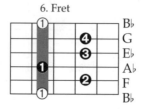

B♭
G
E♭
A♭
F
B♭

B♭°

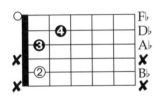

6. Fret

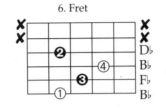

11. Fret

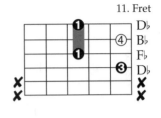

B♭m7♭5

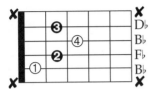

6. Fret

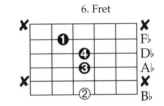

6. Fret

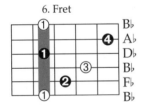

8. Fret

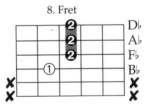

C

C♯/D♭

D

D♯/E♭

E

F

F♯/G♭

G

G♯/A♭

A

A♯/B♭

B

POWER CHORDS

SLASH CHORDS

TRANS- POSING

B♭°7

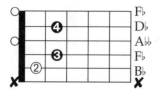
F♭
D♭
A♭♭
F♭
B♭

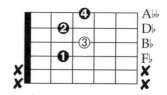
A♭♭
D♭
B♭
F♭

6. Fret
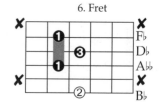
F♭
D♭
A♭♭
B♭

5. Fret
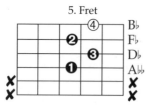
B♭
F♭
D♭
A♭♭

6. Fret
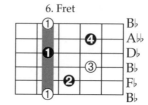
B♭
A♭♭
D♭
B♭
F♭
B♭

8. Fret
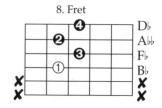
D♭
A♭♭
F♭
B♭

13. Fret
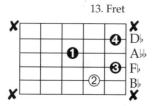
D♭
A♭♭
F♭
B♭

B♭+

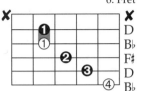

6. Fret	8. Fret	13. Fret

B♭sus4

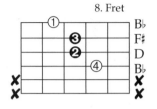

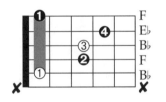

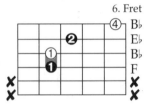

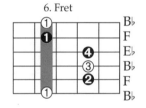

8. Fret

B♭sus2

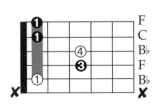

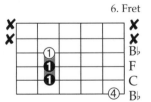

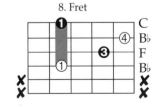

C

C♯/D♭

D

D♯/E♭

E

F

F♯/G♭

G

G♯/A♭

A

A♯/B♭

B

POWER CHORDS

SLASH CHORDS

TRANS-POSING

B

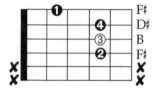
F#
D#
B
F#

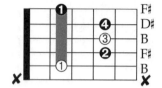
F#
D#
B
F#
B

4. Fret
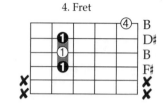
B
D#
B
F#

7. Fret
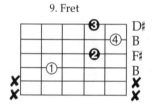
D#
B
F#
D#
B

9. Fret
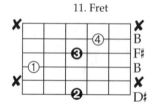
B
F#
D#
B

7. Fret
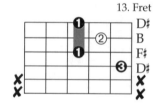
B
F#
D#
B
F#
B

9. Fret
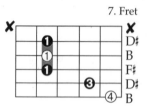
D#
B
F#
B

11. Fret
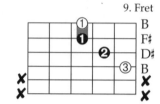
B
F#
B
D#

13. Fret
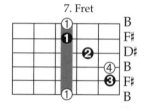
D#
B
F#
D#

14. Fret
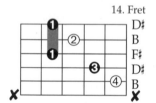
D#
B
F#
D#
B

B6

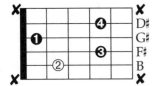
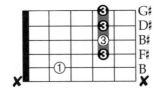
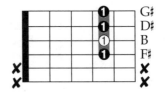

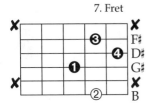
7. Fret

9. Fret (no 5)

9. Fret

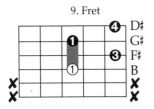
9. Fret

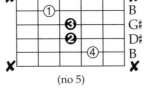
14. Fret (no 5)

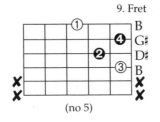
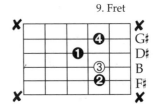

B^{6}_{9}

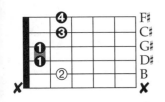

7. Fret

9. Fret (no 5)

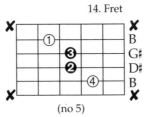
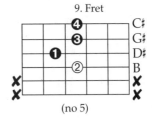

14. Fret

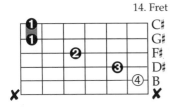
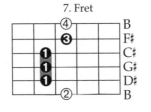

C

C♯/D♭

D

D♯/E♭

E

F

F♯/G♭

G

G♯/A♭

A

A♯/B♭

B

POWER CHORDS

SLASH CHORDS

TRANS-POSING

Bmaj7

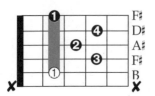

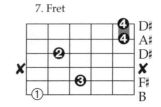
4. Fret

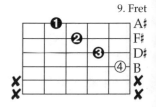
9. Fret

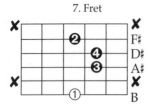
7. Fret

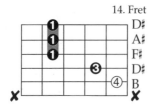
7. Fret

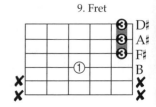
9. Fret

14. Fret

Bmaj13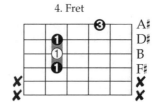

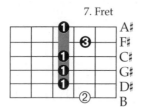
7. Fret

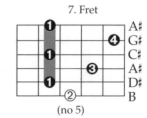
7. Fret

(no 5)

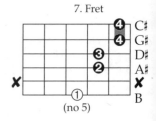
7. Fret

(no 5)

Bmaj9

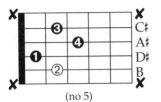

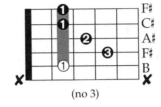

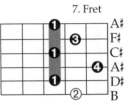

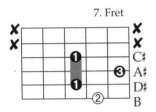

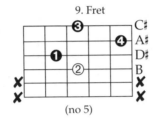

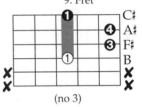

Bmaj9♯11

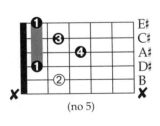

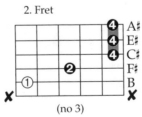

C

C♯/D♭

D

D♯/E♭

E

F

F♯/G♭

G

G♯/A♭

A

A♯/B♭

B

POWER CHORDS

SLASH CHORDS

TRANS-POSING

Bmaj7+

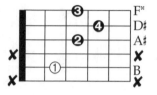

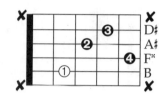

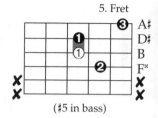

5. Fret

(♯5 in bass)

9. Fret

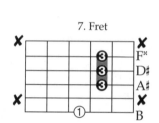

7. Fret

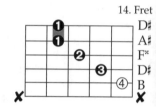

14. Fret

Bmaj7♭5

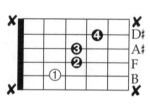

7. Fret

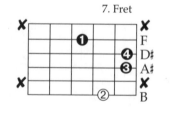

9. Fret

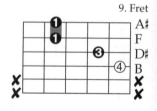

9. Fret

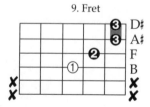

Bmaj13(no9)

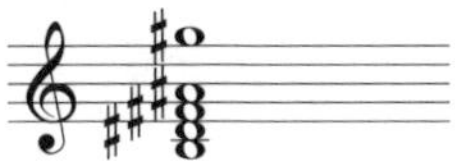

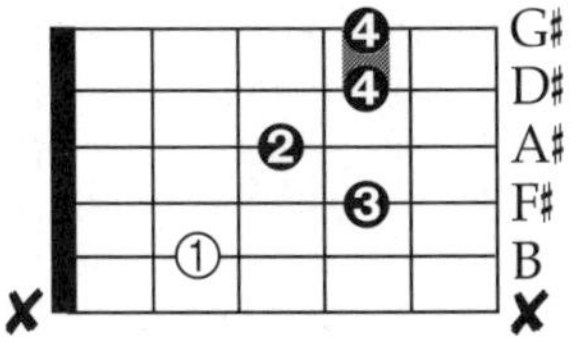

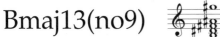

9. Fret

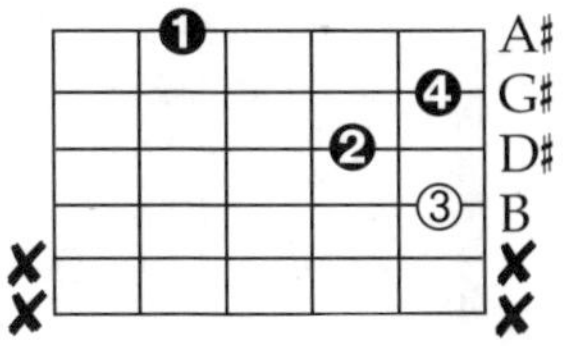

(no 5)

7. Fret

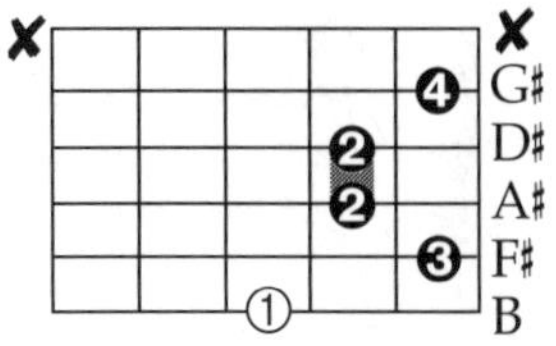

14. Fret

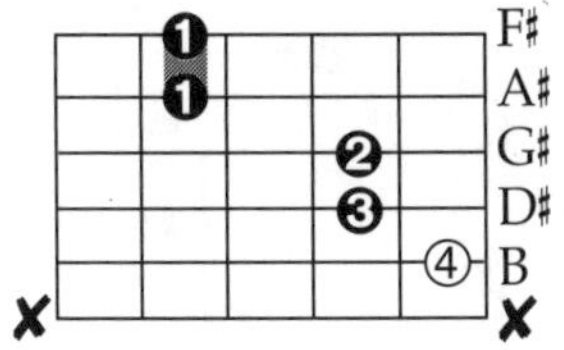

(no 5)

Badd9

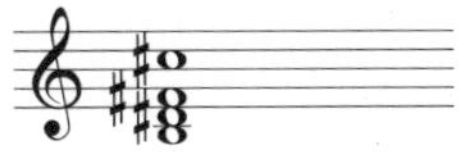

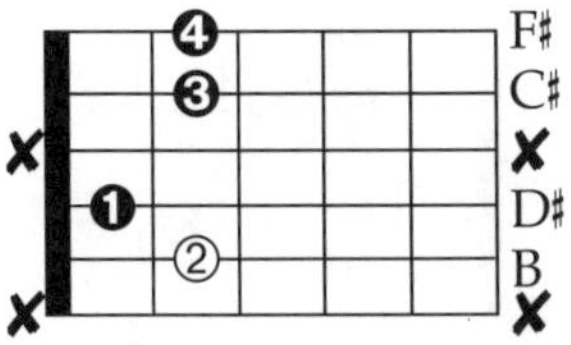

2. Fret

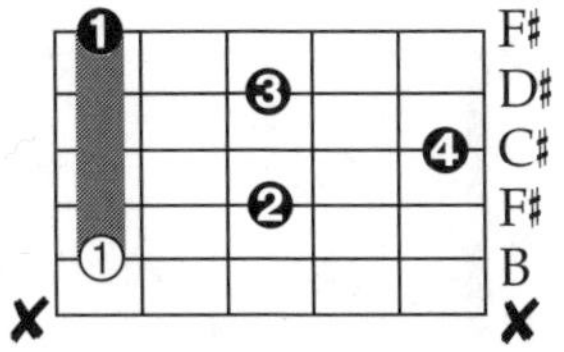

9. Fret

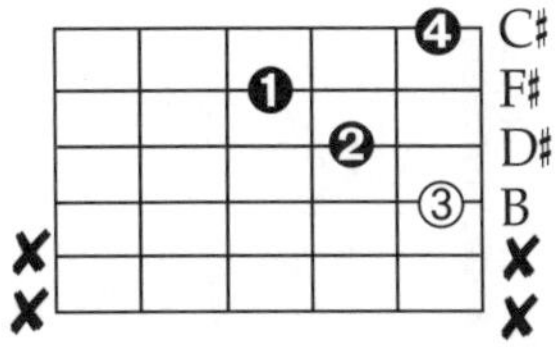

7. Fret

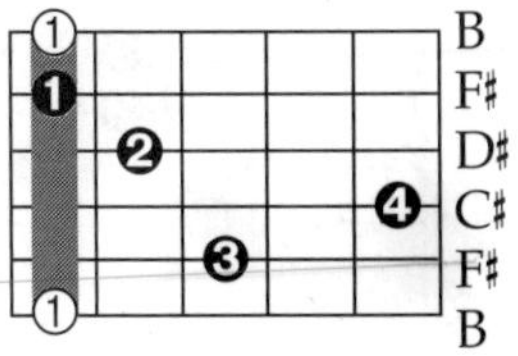

14. Fret

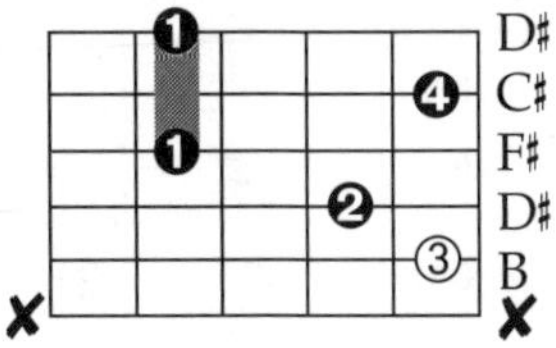

Bm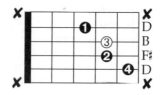

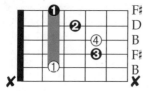

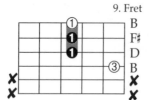

7. Fret

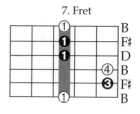

9. Fret

9. Fret

12. Fret

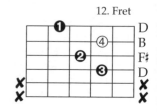

Bm7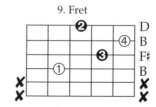

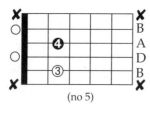

(no 5)

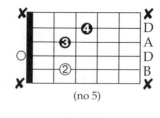

(no 5)

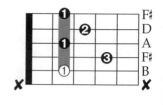

7. Fret

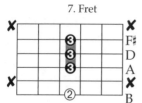

7. Fret

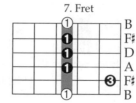

9. Fret

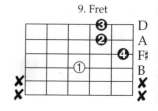

Bm6

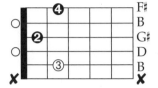
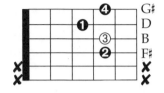
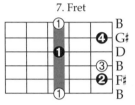
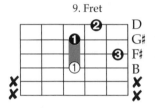

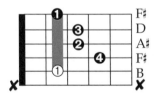
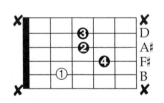
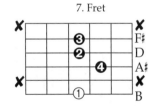

Bm(maj7)

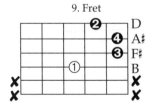
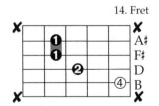
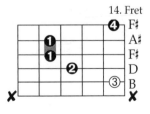

C

C♯/D♭

D

D♯/E♭

E

F

F♯/G♭

G

G♯/A♭

A

A♯/B♭

B

POWER
CHORDS

SLASH
CHORDS

TRANS-
POSING

Bm add9

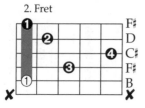

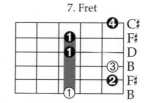

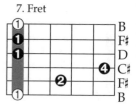

Bm9

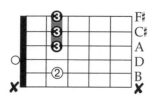

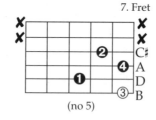

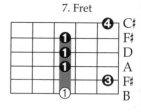

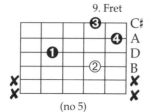

Bm(maj9)

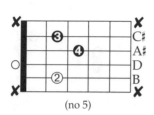

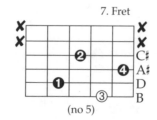

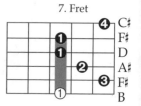

Bm $^6_9$

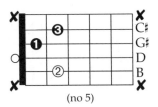
(no 5)

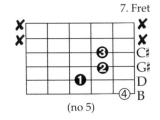
7. Fret
(no 5)

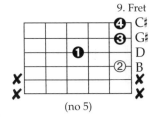
9. Fret
(no 5)

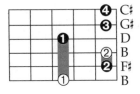
7. Fret

Bm11(no9)

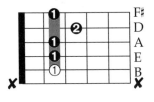

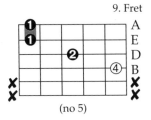
9. Fret
(no 5)

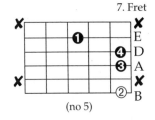
7. Fret
(no 5)

Bm11

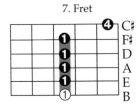
7. Fret

C
C#/Db
D
D#/Eb
E
F
F#/Gb
G
G#/Ab
A
A#/Bb
B
POWER CHORDS
SLASH CHORDS
TRANS POSING

B7

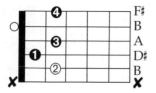

F#
B
A
D#
B

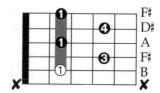

F#
D#
A
F#
B

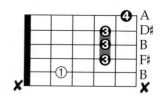

A
D#
B
F#
B

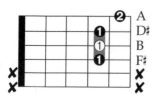

A
D#
B
F#

7. Fret

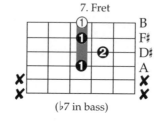

B
F#
D#
A

(♭7 in bass)

7. Fret

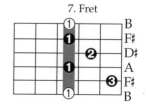

B
F#
D#
A
B

9. Fret

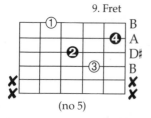

B
A
D#
B

(no 5)

7. Fret

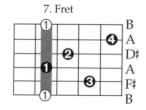

B
A
D#
A
F#
B

9. Fret

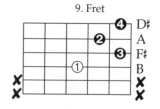

D#
A
F#
B

13. Fret

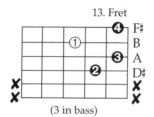

F#
B
A
D#

(3 in bass)

C
C#/D♭
D
D#/E♭
E
F
F#/G♭
G
G#/A♭
A
A#/B♭
B
POWER CHORDS
SLASH CHORDS
TRANS-POSING

B9

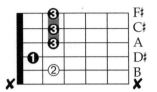

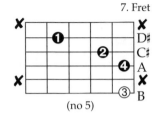

7. Fret

(no 5)

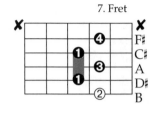

7. Fret

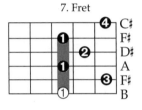

7. Fret

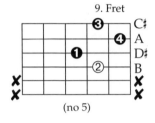

9. Fret

(no 5)

B13

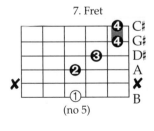

(no 5)

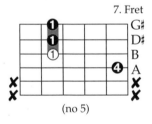

7. Fret

(no 5)

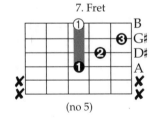

7. Fret

(no 5)

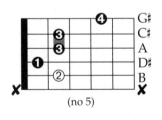

7. Fret

(no 5)

C
C#/Db
D
D#/Eb
E
F
F#/Gb
G
G#/Ab
A
A#/Bb
B
POWER CHORDS
SLASH CHORDS
TRANS-POSING

B7♭9

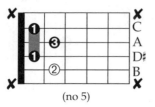
(no 5)

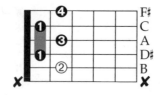

7. Fret
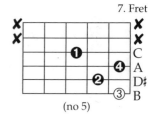
(no 5)

9. Fret
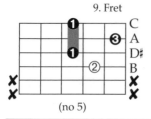
(no 5)

B7♯9

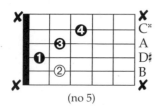
(no 5)

7. Fret
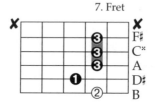

7. Fret
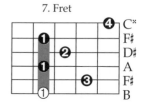

9. Fret
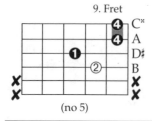
(no 5)

B13♭9

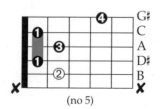
(no 5)

7. Fret
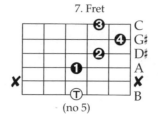
(no 5)

B7+

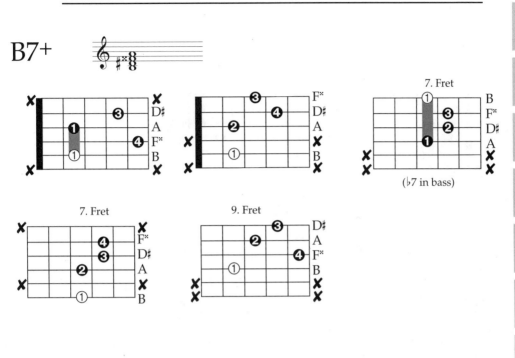

B7♭5

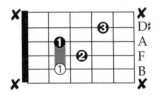
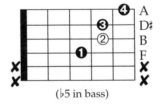
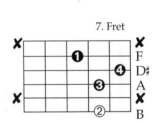

(♭5 in bass)

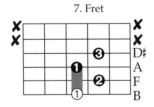
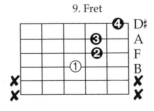

C

C♯/D♭

D

D♯/E♭

E

F

F♯/G♭

G

G♯/A♭

A

A♯/B♭

B

POWER CHORDS

SLASH CHORDS

TRANS-POSING

C
C♯/D♭
D
D♯/E♭
E
F
F♯/G♭
G
G♯/A♭
A
A♯/B♭
B
POWER CHORDS
SLASH CHORDS
TRANS-POSING

B7 ♭9 ♯5

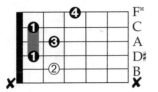

7. Fret

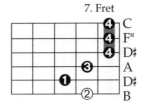

B7 ♯9 ♯5

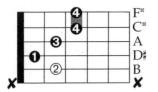

7. Fret

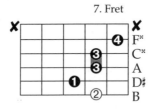

B9♯11

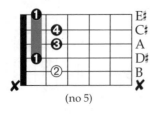

(no 5)

7. Fret

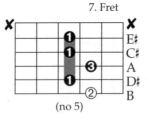

(no 5)

B9+

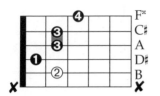

7. Fret

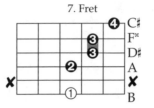

B7sus4

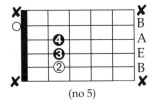
(no 5)

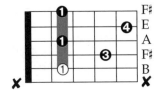

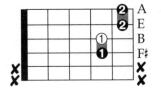

7. Fret

9. Fret

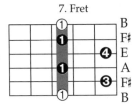

B9sus4

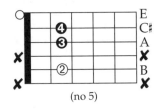
(no 5)

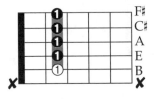

7. Fret

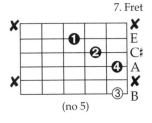
(no 5)

9. Fret

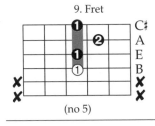
(no 5)

B13sus4

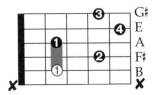

7. Fret

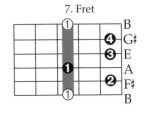

C

C♯/D♭

D

D♯/E♭

E

F

F♯/G♭

G

G♯/A♭

A

A♯/B♭

B

POWER CHORDS

SLASH CHORDS

TRANS-POSING

B°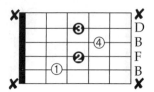

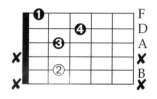

7. Fret

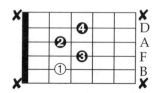

12. Fret

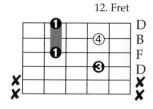

Bm7♭5

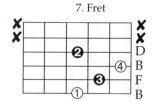

7. Fret

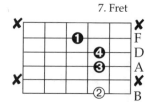

7. Fret   9. Fret

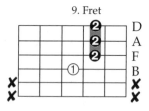

B°7

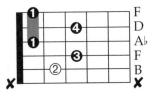
F
D
A♭
F
B

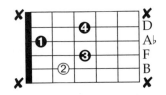
D
A♭
F
B

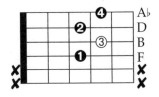
A♭
D
B
F

7. Fret
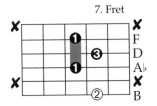
F
D
A♭
B

6. Fret
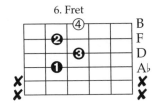
B
F
D
A♭

7. Fret
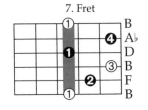
B
A♭
D
B
F
B

9. Fret
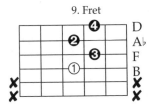
D
A♭
F
B

C
C♯/D♭
D
D♯/E♭
E
F
F♯/G♭
G
G♯/A♭
A
A♯/B♭
B
POWER CHORDS
SLASH CHORDS
TRANS- POSING

B+

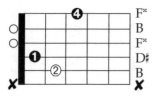
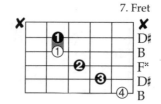
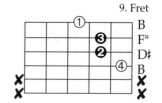

Bsus4

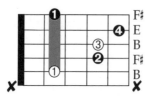
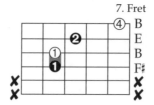
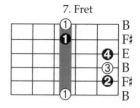

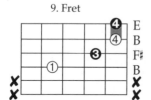

Bsus2

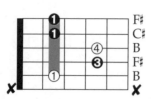
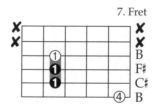
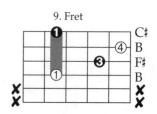

E5 (E/Em)

 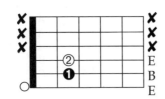

F5 (F/Fm)

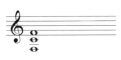 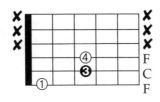

F#5 (F#/F#m)

 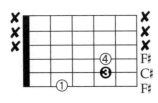

G5 (G/Gm)

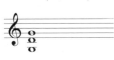 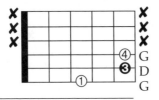

Ab5 (Ab/Abm)

 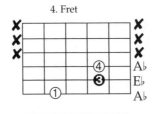

A5 (A/Am)

 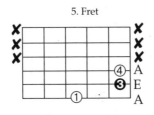

C

C#/Db

D

D#/Eb

E

F

F#/Gb

G

G#/Ab

A

A#/Bb

B

POWER CHORDS

SLASH CHORDS

TRANS-POSING

B♭5 (B♭/B♭m)

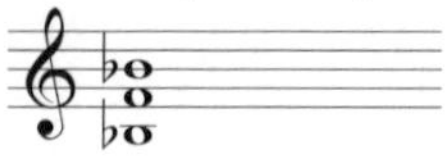

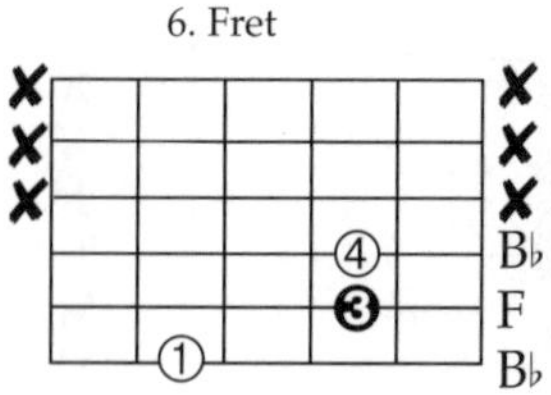
6. Fret
4
3
1
B♭
F
B♭

B5 (B/Bm)

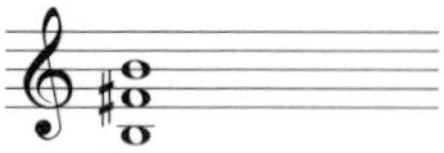

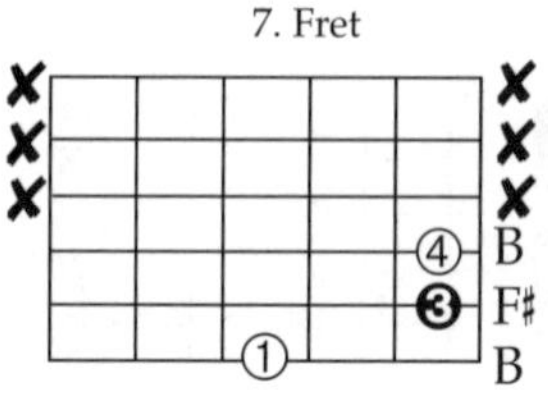
7. Fret
4
3
1
B
F♯
B

C5 (C/Cm)

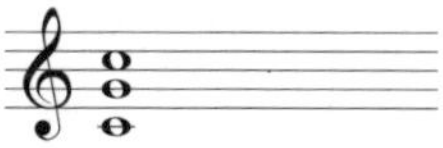

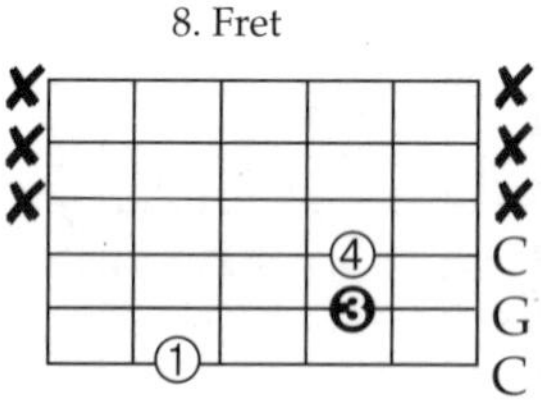
8. Fret
4
3
1
C
G
C

C♯5 (C♯/C♯m)

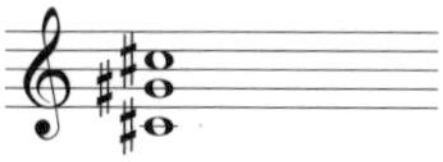

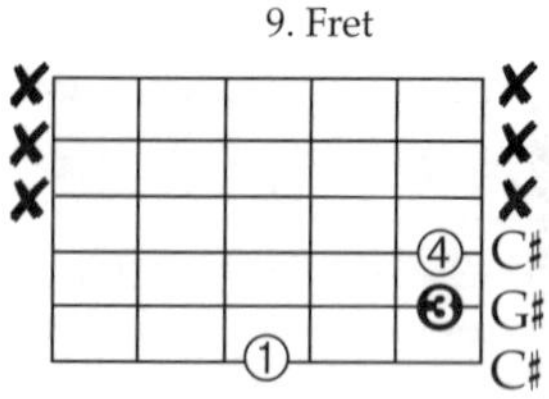
9. Fret
4
3
1
C♯
G♯
C♯

D5 (D/Dm)

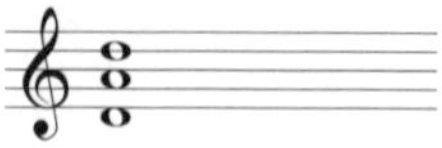

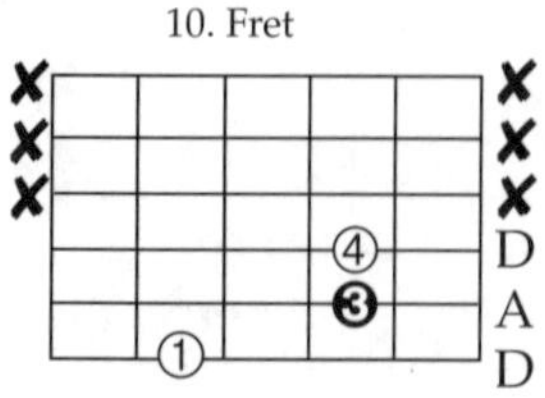
10. Fret
4
3
1
D
A
D

E♭5 (E♭/E♭m)

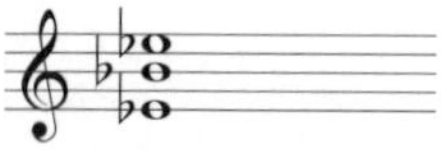

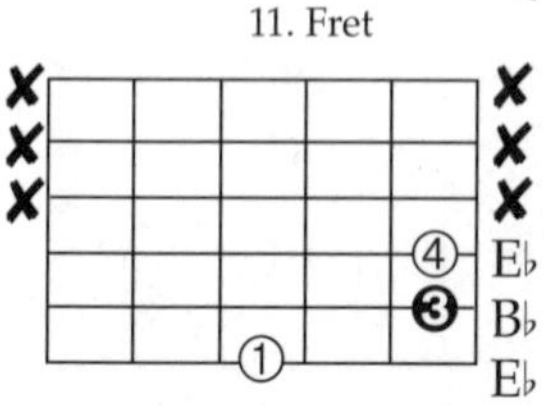
11. Fret
4
3
1
E♭
B♭
E♭

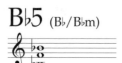

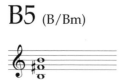

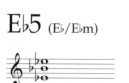

A5 (A/Am)

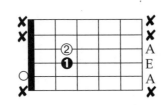

Bb5 (Bb/Bbm)

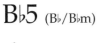

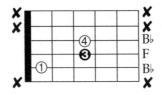

B5 (B/Bm)

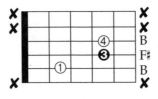

C5 (C/Cm)

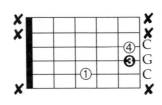

C#5 (C#/C#m)

4. Fret

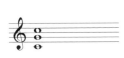

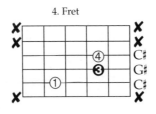

Db5 (D/Dm)

5. Fret

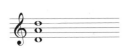

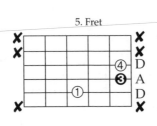

C
C#/Db
D
D#/Eb
E
F
F#/Gb
G
G#/Ab
A
A#/Bb
B
POWER CHORDS
SLASH CHORDS
TRANS-POSING

E♭5 (E♭/E♭m)

6. Fret

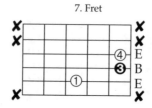

E5 (E/Em)

7. Fret

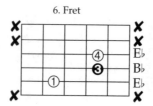

F5 (F/Fm)

8. Fret

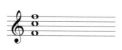

F♯5 (F♯/F♯m)

9. Fret

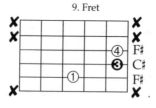

G5 (G/Gm)

10. Fret

A♭5 (A♭/A♭m)

11. Fret

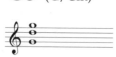

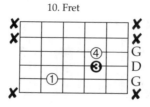

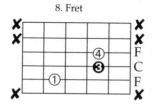

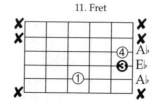

D5 (D/Dm)

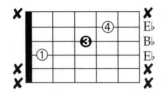

E♭5 (E♭/E♭m)

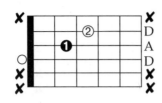

E5 (E/Em)

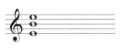

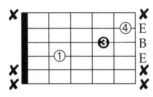

F5 (F/Fm)

3. Fret

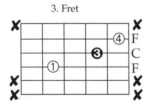

F♯5 (F♯/F♯m)

4. Fret

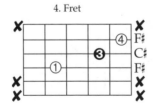

G5 (G/Gm)

5. Fret

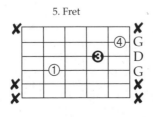

C

C♯/D♭

D

D♯/E♭

E

F

F♯/G♭

G

G♯/A♭

A

A♯/B♭

B

POWER CHORDS

SLASH CHORDS

TRANS-POSING

A♭5 (A♭/A♭m)

6. Fret
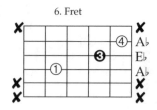
A♭
E♭
A♭

A5 (A/Am)

7. Fret
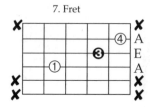
A
E
A

B♭5 (B♭/B♭m)

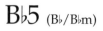

8. Fret
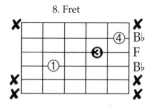
B♭
F
B♭

B5 (B/Bm)

9. Fret
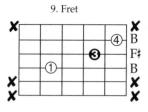
B
F♯
B

C5 (C/Cm)

10. Fret
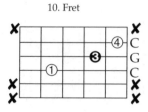
C
G
C

C♯5 (C♯/C♯m)

11. Fret
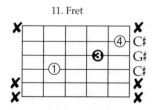
C♯
G♯
C♯

C
C♯/D♭
D
D♯/E♭
E
F
F♯/G♭
G
G♯/A♭
A
A♯/B♭
B
POWER CHORDS
SLASH CHORDS
TRANS-POSING

Esus4

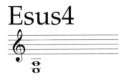
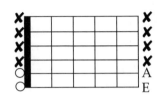

Fsus4

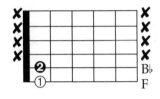

F#sus4

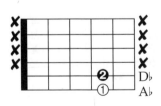

Gsus4

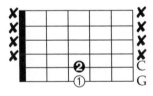

A♭sus4

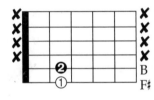

Asus4

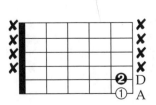

C

C#/D♭

D

D#/E♭

E

F

F#/G♭

G

G#/A♭

A

A#/B♭

B

POWER CHORDS

SLASH CHORDS

TRANS-POSING

B♭sus4

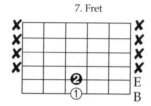

6. Fret

E♭
B♭

Bsus4

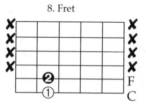

7. Fret

E
B

Csus4

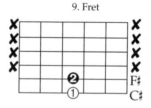

8. Fret

F
C

C♯sus4

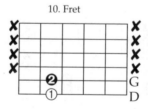

9. Fret

F♯
C♯

Dsus4

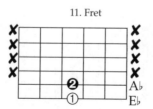

10. Fret

G
D

E♭sus4

11. Fret

A♭
E♭

Asus4

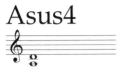

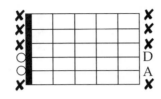

B♭sus4

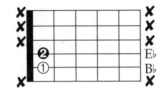

Bsus4

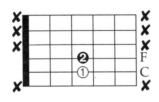

Csus4

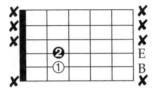

C♯sus4

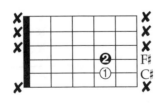

Dsus4

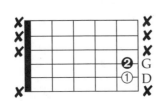

C

C♯/D♭

D

D♯/E♭

E

F

F♯/G♭

G

G♯/A♭

A

A♯/B♭

B

POWER CHORDS

SLASH CHORDS

TRANS-POSING

Ebsus4

6. Fret

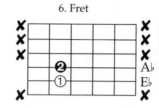

Ab
Eb

Esus4

7. Fret

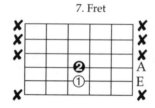

A
E

Fsus4

8. Fret

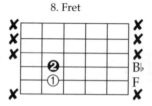

Bb
F

F#sus4

9. Fret

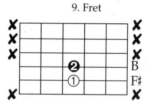

B
F#

Gsus4

10. Fret

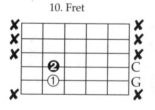

C
G

Absus4

11. Fret

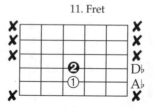

Db
Ab

C
C#/Db
D
D#/Eb
E
F
F#/Gb
G
G#/Ab
A
A#/Bb
B
POWER CHORDS
SLASH CHORDS
TRANS-POSING

Dsus4

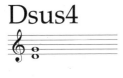
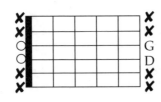

Ebsus4

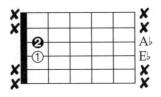

Esus4

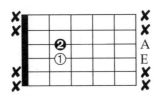

Fsus4

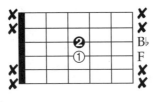

F#sus4

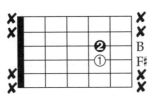

Gsus4

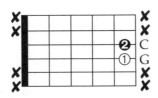

C

C#/Db

D

D#/Eb

E

F

F#/Gb

G

G#/Ab

A

A#/Bb

B

POWER CHORDS

SLASH CHORDS

TRANS- POSING

C

C#/Db

D

D#/Eb

E

F

F#/Gb

G

G#/Ab

A

A#/Bb

B

POWER CHORDS

SLASH CHORDS

TRANS-POSING

A♭sus4

6. Fret

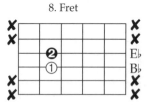

Db
Ab

Asus4

7. Fret

D
A

B♭sus4

8. Fret

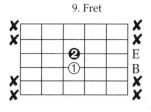

Eb
Bb

Bsus4

9. Fret

E
B

Csus4

10. Fret

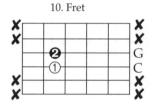

G
C

C#sus4

11. Fret

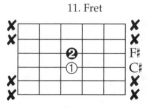

F#
C#

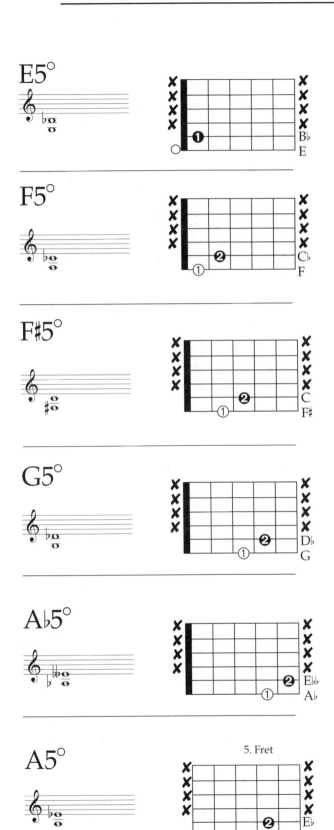

C

C#/Db

D

D#/Eb

E

F

F#/Gb

G

G#/Ab

A

A#/Bb

B

POWER CHORDS

SLASH CHORDS

TRANS-POSING

C
C#/Db
D
D#/Eb
E
F
F#/Gb
G
G#/Ab
A
A#/Bb
B
POWER CHORDS
SLASH CHORDS
TRANS-POSING

Bb5°

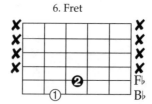

6. Fret

B5°

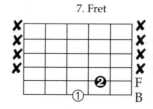

7. Fret

C5°

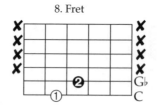

8. Fret

C#5°

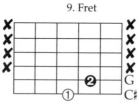

9. Fret

D5°

10. Fret

Eb5°

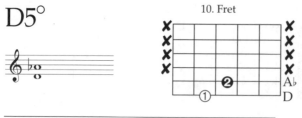

11. Fret

A5°

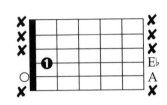

Eb
A

Bb5°

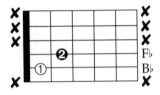

Fb
Bb

B5°

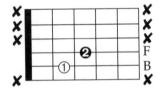

F
B

C5°

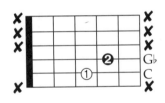

Gb
C

C#5°

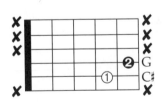

G
C#

D5°

5. Fret

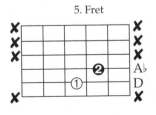

Ab
D

C

C#/Db

D

D#/Eb

E

F

F#/Gb

G

G#/Ab

A

A#/Bb

B

POWER CHORDS

SLASH CHORDS

TRANS-POSING

E♭5°

6. Fret

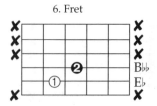

B♭♭
E♭

E5°

7. Fret

B♭
E

F5°

8. Fret

C♭
F

F♯5°

9. Fret

C
F♯

G5°

10. Fret

D♭
G

A♭5°

11. Fret

E♭♭
A♭

D5°

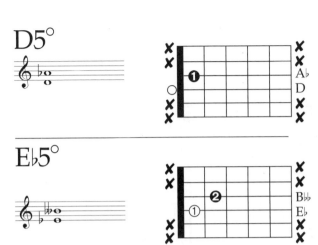

E♭5°

E5°

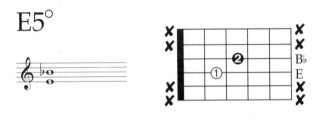

F5°

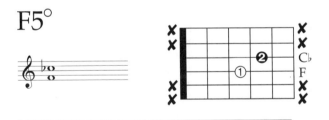

F#5°

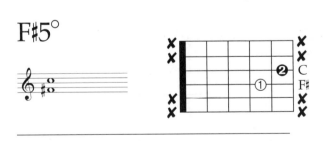

G5°

5. Fret

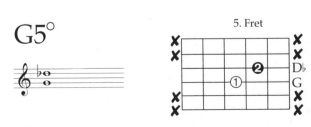

C

C♯/D♭

D

D♯/E♭

E

F

F♯/G♭

G

G♯/A♭

A

A♯/B♭

B

POWER CHORDS

SLASH CHORDS

TRANS-POSING

A♭5°

6. Fret

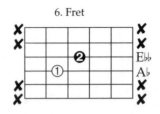

E♭♭
A♭

A5°

7. Fret

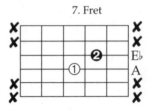

E♭
A

B♭5°

8. Fret

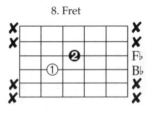

F♭
B♭

B5°

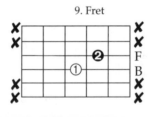

9. Fret

F
B

C5°

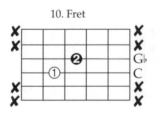

10. Fret

G♭
C

C♯5°

11. Fret

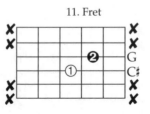

G
C♯

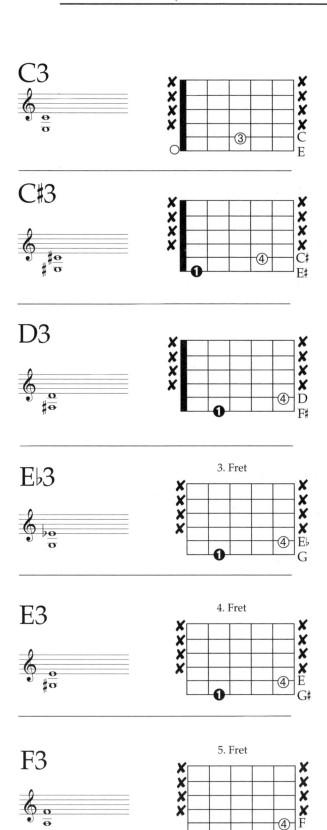

C3

C#3

D3

Eb3
3. Fret

E3
4. Fret

F3
5. Fret

C

C#/Db

D

D#/Eb

E

F

F#/Gb

G

G#/Ab

A

A#/Bb

B

POWER
CHORDS

SLASH
CHORDS

TRANS-
POSING

F#3

6. Fret

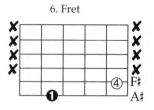

F#
A#

G3

7. Fret

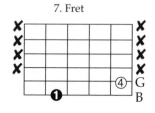

G
B

A♭3

8. Fret

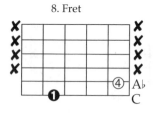

A♭
C

A3

9. Fret

A
C#

B♭3

10. Fret

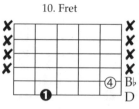

B♭
D

B3

11. Fret

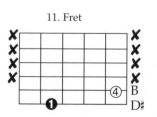

B
D#

C

C#/D♭

D

D#/E♭

E

F

F#/G♭

G

G#/A♭

A

A#/B♭

B

POWER CHORDS

SLASH CHORDS

TRANS-POSING

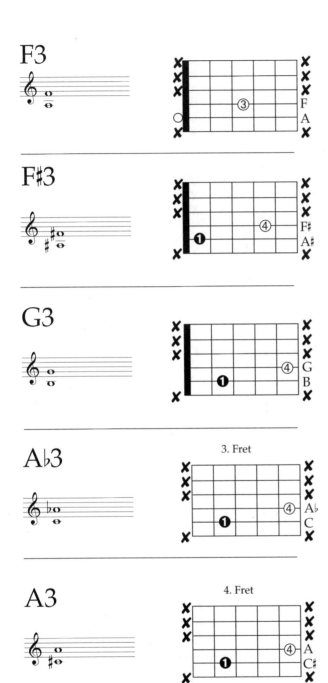

F3

F♯3

G3

A♭3
3. Fret

A3
4. Fret

B♭3
5. Fret

C

C♯/D♭

D

D♯/E♭

E

F

F♯/G♭

G

G♯/A♭

A

A♯/B♭

B

POWER CHORDS

SLASH CHORDS

TRANS-POSING

C

C#/Db

D

D#/Eb

E

F

F#/Gb

G

G#/Ab

A

A#/Bb

B

POWER CHORDS

SLASH CHORDS

TRANS-POSING

B3

6. Fret

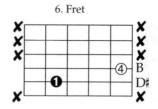

B
D#

C3

7. Fret

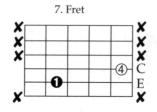

C
E

C#3

8. Fret

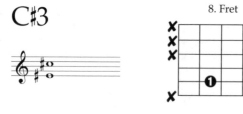

C#
E#

D3

9. Fret

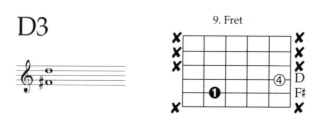

D
F#

Eb3

10. Fret

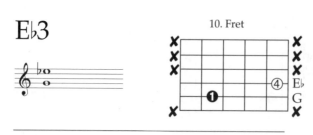

Eb
G

E3

11. Fret

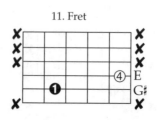

E
G#

B♭3

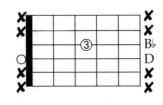

Bb
D

B3

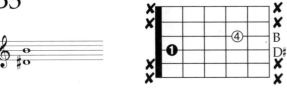
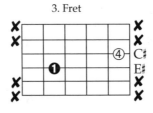

B
D#

C3

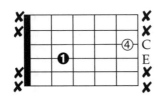

C
E

C#3

3. Fret

C#
E#

D3

4. Fret

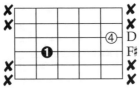

D
F#

E♭3

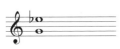

5. Fret

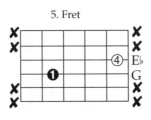

Eb
G

C
C#/D♭
D
D#/E♭
E
F
F#/G♭
G
G#/A♭
A
A#/B♭
B
POWER CHORDS
SLASH CHORDS
TRANS-POSING

E3

6. Fret

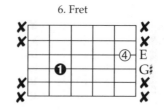

E
G#

F3

7. Fret

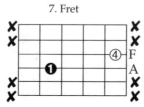

F
A

F#3

8. Fret

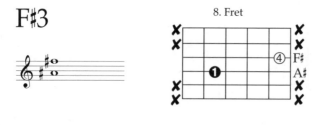

F#
A#

G3

9. Fret

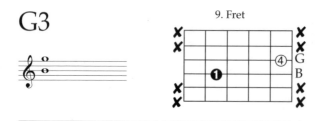

G
B

Ab3

10. Fret

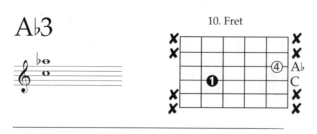

Ab
C

A3

11. Fret

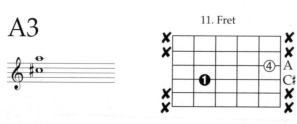

A
C#

C

C#/D♭

D

D#/E♭

E

F

F#/G♭

G

G#/A♭

A

A#/B♭

B

POWER CHORDS

SLASH CHORDS

TRANS-POSING

E6

F6

F#6

G6

A♭6

A6

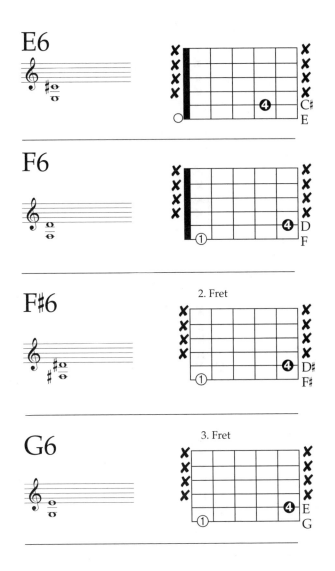

Bb6

6. Fret
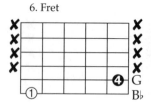
④ G
① Bb

B6

7. Fret
④ G#
B

C6

8. Fret
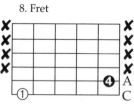
④ A
C

C#6

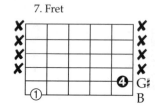

9. Fret
④ A#
C#

D6

10. Fret
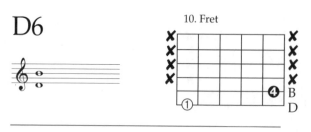
④ B
D

Eb6

11. Fret
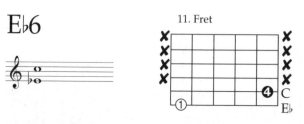
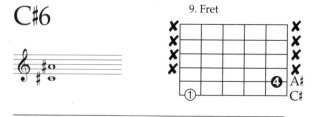
④ C
Eb

C
C#/Db
D
D#/Eb
E
F
F#/Gb
G
G#/Ab
A
A#/Bb
B
POWER CHORDS
SLASH CHORDS
TRANS-POSING

A6

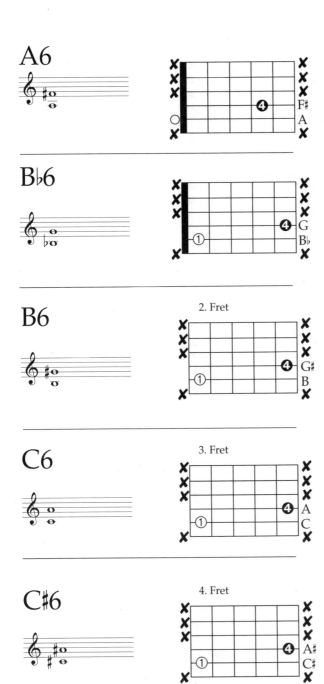

B♭6

B6

2. Fret

C6

3. Fret

C♯6

4. Fret

D6

5. Fret

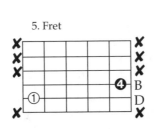

C
C♯/D♭
D
D♯/E♭
E
F
F♯/G♭
G
G♯/A♭
A
A♯/B♭
B
POWER CHORDS
SLASH CHORDS
TRANS-POSING

Eb6

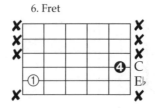

E6

F6

F#6

G6

Ab6

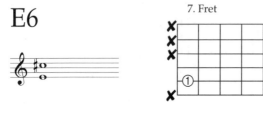

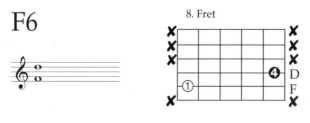

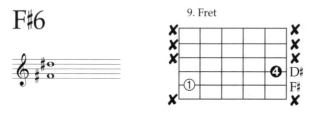

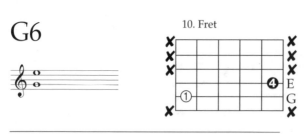

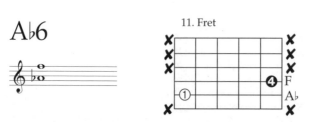

D6

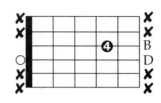

B
D

E♭6

C
E♭

E6

2. Fret

C#
E

F6

3. Fret

D
F

F#6

4. Fret

D#
F#

G6

5. Fret

E
G

C
C#/D♭
D
D#/E♭
E
F
F#/G♭
G
G#/A♭
A
A#/B♭
B
POWER CHORDS
SLASH CHORDS
TRANS-POSING

A♭6

6. Fret

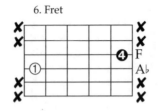

A6

7. Fret

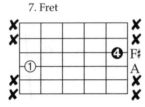

B♭6

8. Fret

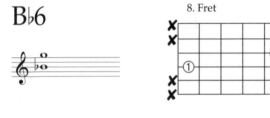

B6

9. Fret

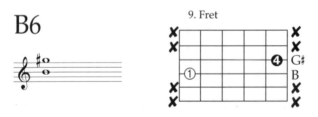

C6

10. Fret

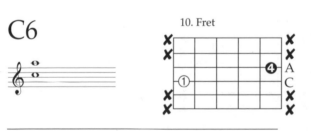

C♯6

11. Fret

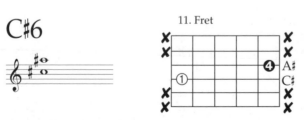

C/C

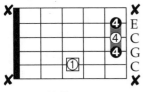

8. Fret

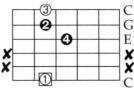

8. Fret

10. Fret

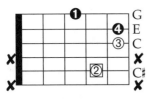

C/C#

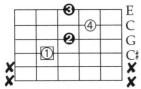

9. Fret

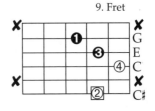

11. Fret

C/D

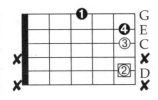

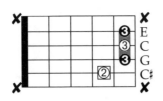

10. Fret

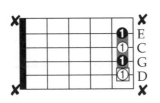

12. Fret

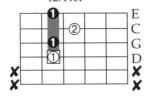

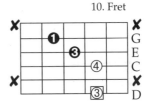

C

C#/Db

D

D#/Eb

E

F

F#/Gb

G

G#/Ab

A

A#/Bb

B

POWER CHORDS

SLASH CHORDS

TRANS- POSING

C/Eb

6. Fret

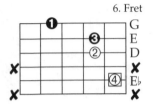
G E D X Eb X

6. Fret

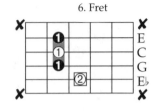
X E C G Eb X

11. Fret

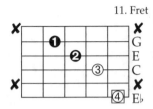
X X G E C X Eb

11. Fret

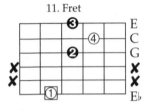
E C G X X Eb

C/E

7. Fret

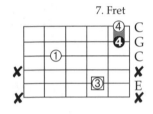
C G C X E X

12. Fret

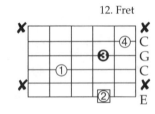
C G C X E

14. Fret

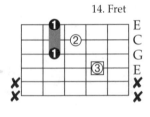
E C G E X X

C/F

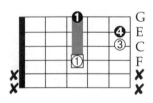
G E C F X X

8. Fret

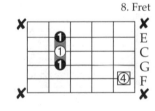
X E C G F X

8. Fret

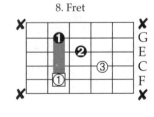
X G E C F X

15. Fret

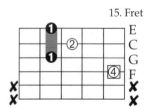
E C G F X X

C/F#

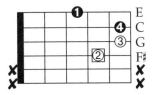

9. Fret

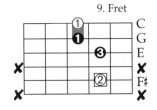

14. Fret

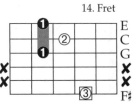

14. Fret

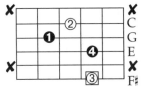

C/G

8. Fret

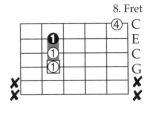

10. Fret

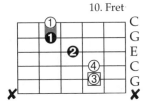

10. Fret

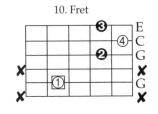

C/Ab

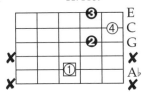

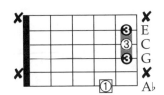

11. Fret

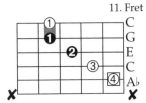

11. Fret

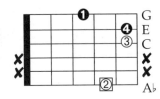

C
C#/Db
D
D#/Eb
E
F
F#/Gb
G
G#/Ab
A
A#/Bb
B
POWER CHORDS
SLASH CHORDS
TRANS-POSING

C/A

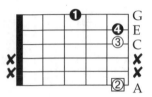

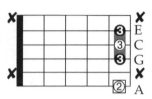

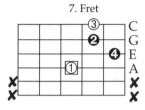

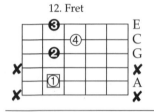

C/Bb

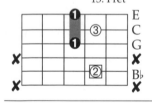

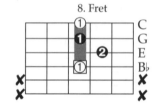

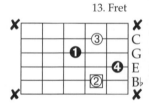

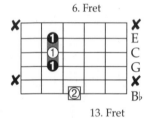

C/B

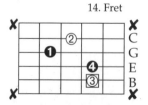

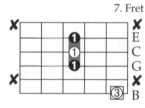

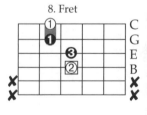

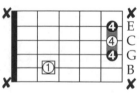

Transposing

Transposing is the process of rewriting a melody, chord or piece of music into a different key. The relative note intervals remain the same. Unlike the piano, where transposing a chord to a different key results in different finger positions, the guitarist keeps the same finger positions and merely moves up or down the fretboard. As an example, we'll take a look at the F major bar chord. As you can see, to transpose this chord to F♯ major it is simply a matter of moving up a half-step, or one fret position. To further transpose to a G major chord, the F♯ major chord is moved up one fret position.

F major

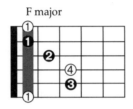

F♯ major

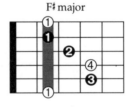

G major etc. →

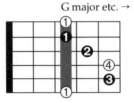

Not all the possible chords on the guitar reflect this simple relationship - this is particularly not true for chords in the first five frets of the instrument where it becomes necessary to alter the fingering. However, as you become more familiar with this book, you will notice that the majority of chords can be transposed in this manner.

C

C♯/D♭

D

D♯/E♭

E

F

F♯/G♭

G

G♯/A♭

A

A♯/B♭

B

POWER
CHORDS

SLASH
CHORDS

TRANS-
POSING